Ikenaga 2 Jos Leys

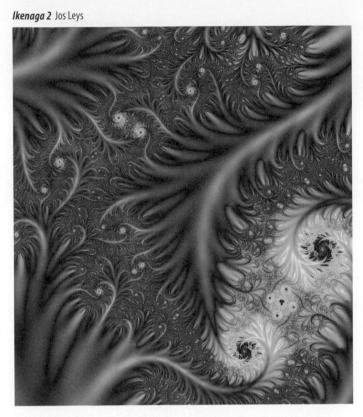

"A relatively simple formula can generate immensely complex images." – **Jos Leys**

Investigations
IN NUMBER, DATA, AND SPACE®

Editorial offices: Glenview, Illinois • Parsippany, New Jersey • New York, New York
Sales offices: Boston, Massachusetts • Duluth, Georgia
Glenview, Illinois • Coppell, Texas • Sacramento, California • Mesa, Arizona

The Investigations curriculum was developed by TERC, Cambridge, MA.

This material is based on work supported by the National Science Foundation ("NSF") under Grant No.ESI-0095450. Any opinions, findings, and conclusions or recommendations expressed in this material are those of the author(s) and do not necessarily reflect the views of the National Science Foundation.

ISBN: 0-328-24090-7

ISBN: 978-0-328-24090-6

7 8 9 10-V057-15 14 13 12 11 10 09
CC:N2

Math Words and Ideas

Number and Operations

Contents

Contents

Games

The **Student Math Handbook** is a reference book. It has two sections.

Math Words and Ideas

These pages illustrate important math words and ideas that you have been learning about in math class. You can use these pages to think about or review a math topic. Important terms are identified and related problems are provided.

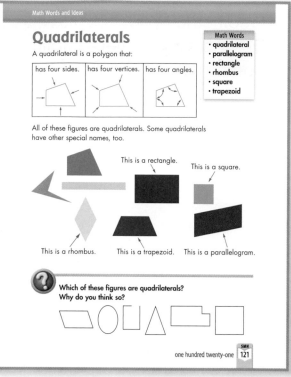

▲ Student Math Handbook, p. 121

Games

You can use the Games pages to go over game rules during class or at home. They also list the materials and recording sheets needed to play each game.

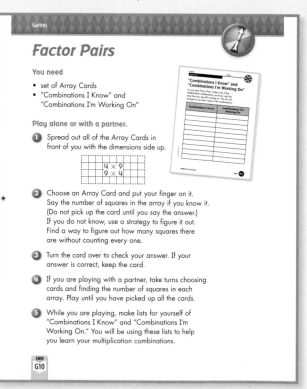

▲ Student Math Handbook, p. G10

Daily Practice and Homework pages list useful *Student Math Handbook* (SMH) pages.

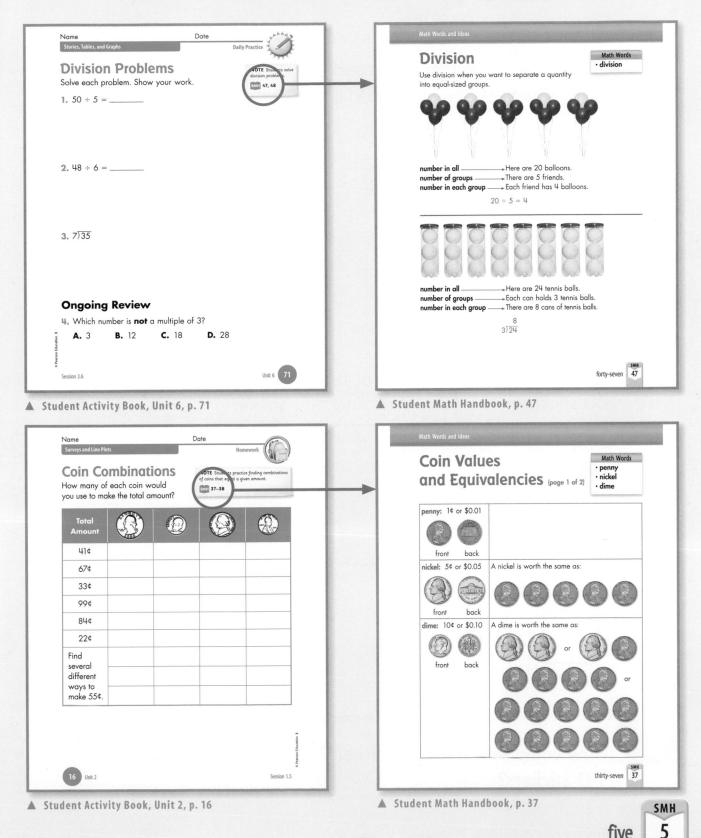

Name _____ Date _____

Stories, Tables, and Graphs

Daily Practice

Division Problems

Solve each problem. Show your work.

NOTE Students solve division problems.
SMH 47, 48

1. 50 ÷ 5 = _____

2. 48 ÷ 6 = _____

3. 7)‾35‾

Ongoing Review

4. Which number is **not** a multiple of 3?

A. 3   B. 12   C. 18   D. 28

© Pearson Education 3

Session 3.6

Unit 6   71

▲ Student Activity Book, Unit 6, p. 71

Math Words and Ideas

Division

Math Words
• division

Use division when you want to separate a quantity into equal-sized groups.

number in all ⟶ Here are 20 balloons.
number of groups ⟶ There are 5 friends.
number in each group ⟶ Each friend has 4 balloons.

20 ÷ 5 = 4

number in all ⟶ Here are 24 tennis balls.
number of groups ⟶ Each can holds 3 tennis balls.
number in each group ⟶ There are 8 cans of tennis balls.

8
3)‾24‾

forty-seven   SMH 47

▲ Student Math Handbook, p. 47

Name _____ Date _____

Surveys and Line Plots

Homework

Coin Combinations

How many of each coin would you use to make the total amount?

NOTE Students practice finding combinations of coins that equal a given amount.
SMH 37–38

Total Amount				
41¢				
67¢				
33¢				
99¢				
84¢				
22¢				
Find several different ways to make 55¢.				

© Pearson Education 3

16   Unit 2

Session 1.5

▲ Student Activity Book, Unit 2, p. 16

Math Words and Ideas

Coin Values and Equivalencies (page 1 of 2)

Math Words
• penny
• nickel
• dime

penny: 1¢ or $0.01

front   back

nickel: 5¢ or $0.05   A nickel is worth the same as:

front   back

dime: 10¢ or $0.10   A dime is worth the same as:

front   back

or

or

thirty-seven   SMH 37

▲ Student Math Handbook, p. 37

five   SMH 5

Representing Place Value

Math Words
• **equation**

Sticker Station is a place that sells stickers.

At Sticker Station you can buy single stickers, strips of ten stickers, or sheets of one hundred stickers.

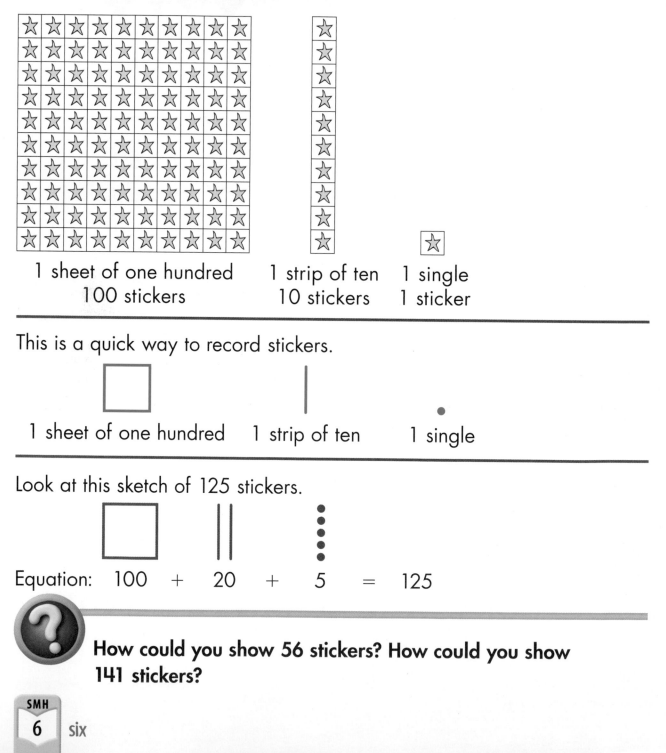

1 sheet of one hundred
100 stickers

1 strip of ten
10 stickers

1 single
1 sticker

This is a quick way to record stickers.

1 sheet of one hundred   1 strip of ten   1 single

Look at this sketch of 125 stickers.

Equation: 100   +   20   +   5   =   125

How could you show 56 stickers? How could you show 141 stickers?

Place Value: Ones, Tens, and Hundreds

(page 1 of 2)

Math Words
• **equal**

10 singles   equal   1 strip of ten

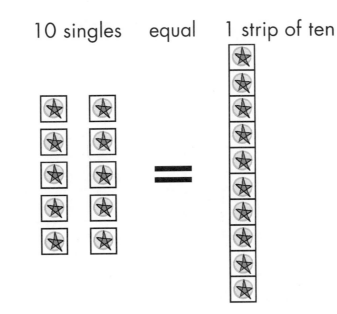

10 strips of ten   equal   1 sheet of one hundred.

Place Value: Ones, Tens, and Hundreds

(page 2 of 2)

Jessica and Carlos went to Sticker Station. They each bought 57 stickers.

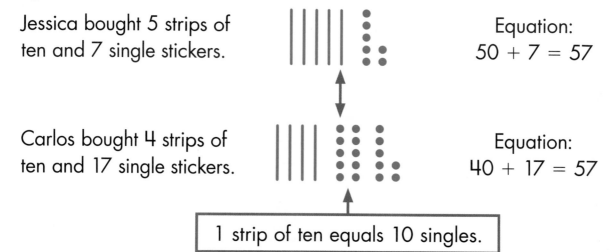

Jessica bought 5 strips of ten and 7 single stickers.

Equation:
50 + 7 = 57

Carlos bought 4 strips of ten and 17 single stickers.

Equation:
40 + 17 = 57

1 strip of ten equals 10 singles.

Kevin and Mia went to Sticker Station. They each bought 128 stickers.

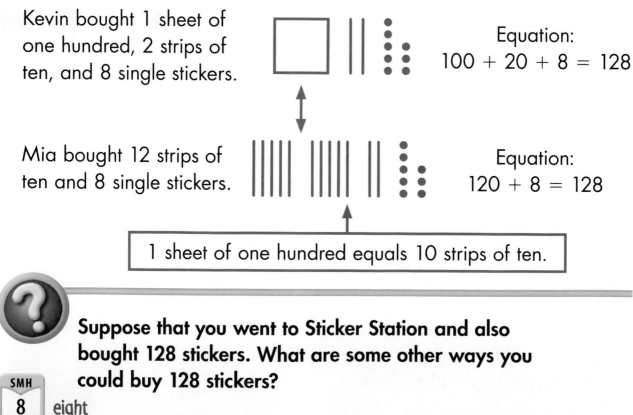

Kevin bought 1 sheet of one hundred, 2 strips of ten, and 8 single stickers.

Equation:
100 + 20 + 8 = 128

Mia bought 12 strips of ten and 8 single stickers.

Equation:
120 + 8 = 128

1 sheet of one hundred equals 10 strips of ten.

Suppose that you went to Sticker Station and also bought 128 stickers. What are some other ways you could buy 128 stickers?

Place Value: Many Ways to Make 145

Four students went to Sticker Station. Each of them bought 145 stickers.

Student	Sheets of 100	Strips of 10	Singles	Equation
Gina bought these stickers.	1	4	5	100 + 40 + 5 = **145**
Adam bought these stickers.	0	14	5	0 + 140 + 5 = **145**
Denzel bought these stickers.	0	13	15	0 + 130 + 15 = **145**
Pilar bought these stickers.	0	12	25	0 + 120 + 25 = **145**

Suppose that you went to Sticker Station and also bought 145 stickers. What are some other ways you could buy 145 stickers?

Place Value: Ones, Tens, Hundreds, and Thousands (page 1 of 2)

(page 1 of 2)

Math Words
- **place value**
- **ones**
- **tens**
- **hundreds**
- **thousands**
- **digit**

The value of a digit changes depending on its place in a number.

_____ ,	_____	_____	_____
thousands	hundreds	tens	ones

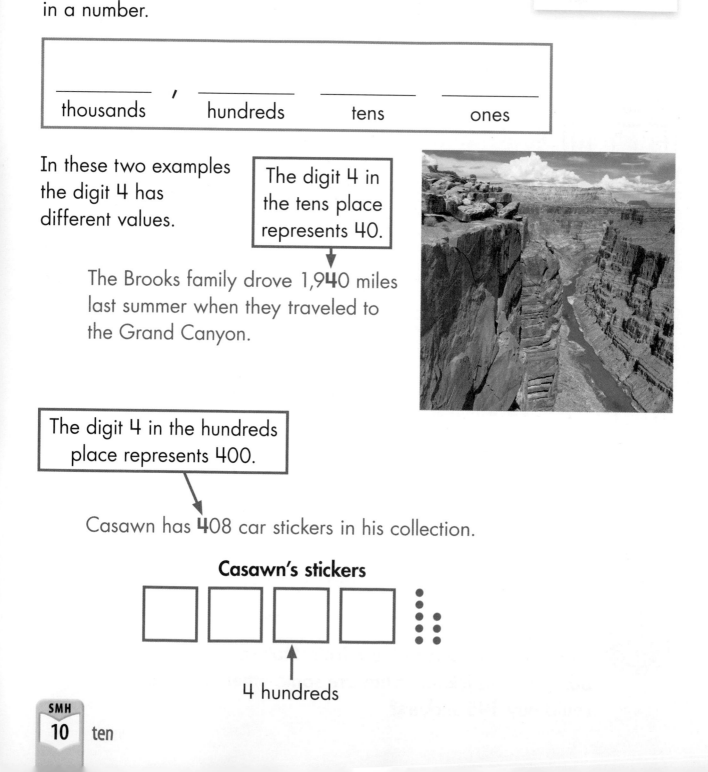

In these two examples the digit 4 has different values.

The digit 4 in the tens place represents 40.

The Brooks family drove 1,9**4**0 miles last summer when they traveled to the Grand Canyon.

The digit 4 in the hundreds place represents 400.

Casawn has **4**08 car stickers in his collection.

Casawn's stickers

4 hundreds

Place Value: Ones, Tens, Hundreds, and Thousands (page 2 of 2)

Look at the values of the digits in these numbers.

408 (four hundred eight)

The digit 4 represents 400.
The digit 0 represents 0 (tens).
The digit 8 represents 8.

$$400 + 0 + 8 = 408$$

1,940 (one thousand, nine hundred forty)

The digit 1 represents 1,000.
The digit 9 represents 900.
The digit 4 represents 40.
The digit 0 represents 0 (ones).

$$1,000 + 900 + 40 + 0 = 1,940$$

?

What are the values of the digits in these numbers?
325   1,867

An Addition Situation

In this addition problem, two groups of stickers are combined or joined.

Arthur went to Sticker Station and bought 36 soccer stickers and 44 animal stickers. How many stickers did he buy altogether?

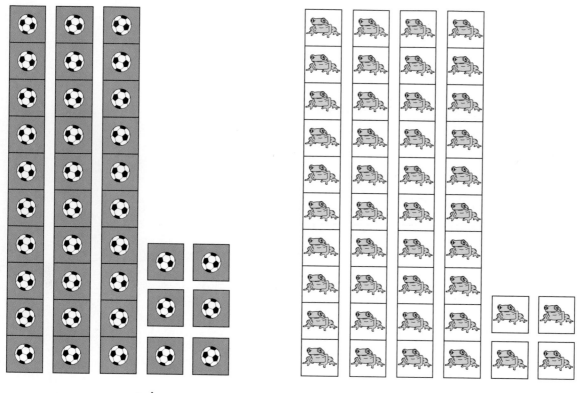

soccer stickers   animal stickers

These equations go with this problem.

$$36 + 44 = ?$$

$$44 + 36 = ?$$

Tools to Represent Addition Problems (page 1 of 3)

On the next few pages, you will see some of the tools you can use to represent addition problems such as this one.

Arthur went to Sticker Station and bought 36 soccer stickers and 44 animal stickers. How many stickers did he buy altogether?

$$36 + 44 = 80$$

Cubes

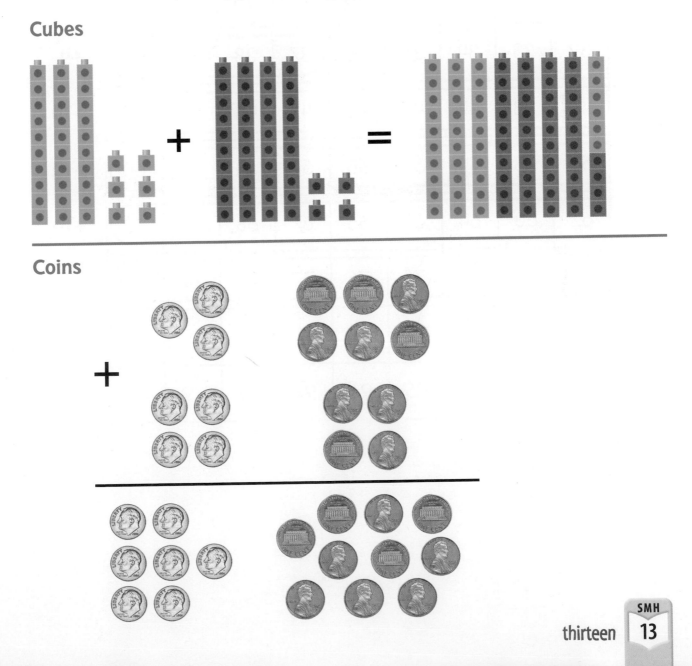

Coins

Tools to Represent Addition Problems (page 2 of 3)

100 Chart

1	2	3	4	5	6	7	8	9	10	
11	12	13	14	15	16	17	18	19	20	
21	22	23	24	25	26	27	28	29	30	
31	32	33	34	35	36	37	38	39	40	+4
41	42	43	44	45	46	47	48	49	50	+10
51	52	53	54	55	56	57	58	59	60	+10
61	62	63	64	65	66	67	68	69	70	+10
71	72	73	74	75	76	77	78	79	80	+10
81	82	83	84	85	86	87	88	89	90	
91	92	93	94	95	96	97	98	99	100	

Tools to Represent Addition Problems (page 3 of 3)

Number Line

This number line is marked by tens from 0 to 100.

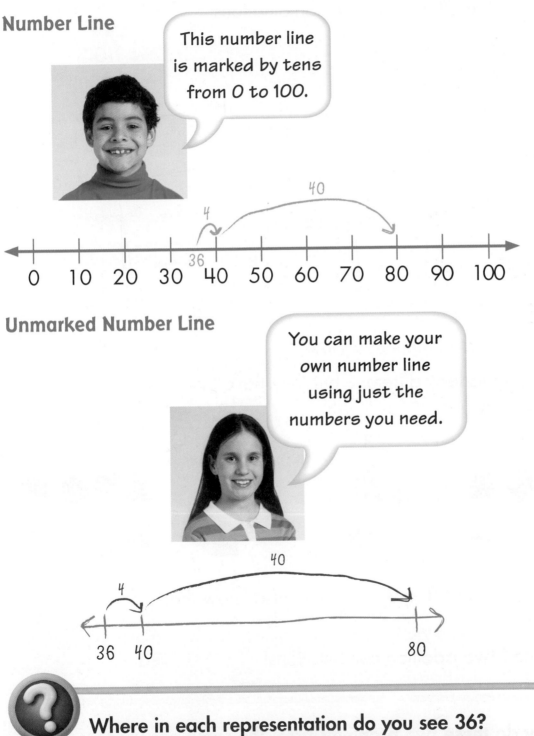

Unmarked Number Line

You can make your own number line using just the numbers you need.

? Where in each representation do you see 36?
Where in each representation do you see 44?
Where in each representation do you see 80?

Addition Combinations

(page 1 of 4)

Math Words
• sum

One of your goals in math class this year is to review and practice all the addition combinations up to 10 + 10.

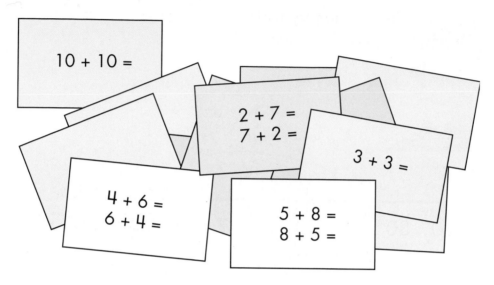

10 + 10 =

2 + 7 =
7 + 2 =

3 + 3 =

4 + 6 =
6 + 4 =

5 + 8 =
8 + 5 =

Learning Two Combinations at a Time

These two problems look different, but they have the same sum.

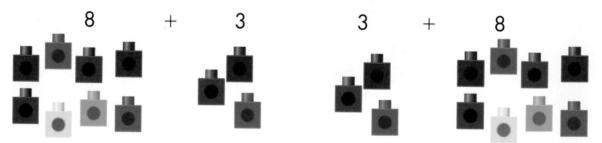

8   +   3   3   +   8

When you know that 8 + 3 = 11, you also know that 3 + 8 = 11.

You've learned two addition combinations!

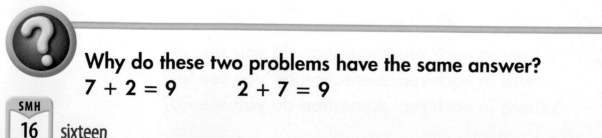

Why do these two problems have the same answer?
7 + 2 = 9   2 + 7 = 9

Addition Combinations

(page 2 of 4)

A helpful way to learn addition combinations is to think about one category at a time. Here are some categories you may have seen before. You probably already know many of these combinations.

Make 10 Combinations

$2 + 8 = 10$
$8 + 2 = 10$

$3 + 7 = 10$
$7 + 3 = 10$

$4 + 6 = 10$
$6 + 4 = 10$

Doubles Combinations

$6 + 6 = 12$

$7 + 7 = 14$

$8 + 8 = 16$

Plus 10 Combinations

$4 + 10 = 14$
$10 + 4 = 14$

$5 + 10 = 15$
$10 + 5 = 15$

$6 + 10 = 16$
$10 + 6 = 16$

Addition Combinations

(page 3 of 4)

Here are some more categories to help you learn more of the addition combinations.

Near-Doubles Combinations

Some combinations are close to a doubles combination you know. Here are two examples.

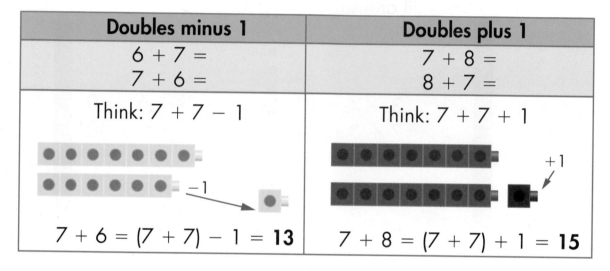

Doubles minus 1	Doubles plus 1
6 + 7 = 7 + 6 =	7 + 8 = 8 + 7 =
Think: 7 + 7 − 1	Think: 7 + 7 + 1
7 + 6 = (7 + 7) − 1 = **13**	7 + 8 = (7 + 7) + 1 = **15**

Plus 9 Combinations

You can learn some combinations by relating them to a plus 10 combination you know. Here are two examples.

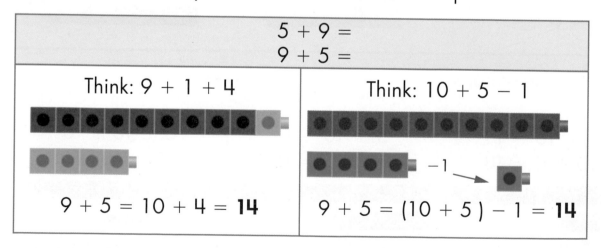

5 + 9 = 9 + 5 =	
Think: 9 + 1 + 4	Think: 10 + 5 − 1
9 + 5 = 10 + 4 = **14**	9 + 5 = (10 + 5) − 1 = **14**

Addition Combinations

(page 4 of 4)

As you practice all the addition combinations, there will be some that you "just know" and others that you are "working on." To practice combinations that are difficult for you to remember, think of a combination that you know as a clue to help you.

Here are some examples. Gil and Ines have different clues to help them solve $5 + 7$.

Gil: *I think of $7 + 7$, and then subtract 2.*

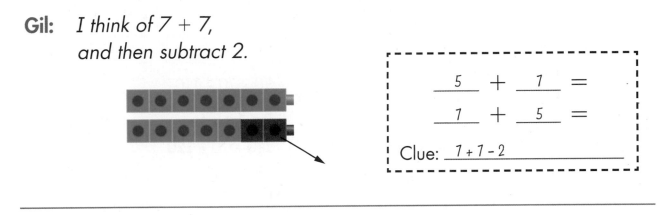

$$\underline{\quad 5 \quad} + \underline{\quad 7 \quad} =$$
$$\underline{\quad 7 \quad} + \underline{\quad 5 \quad} =$$

Clue: $\underline{7 + 7 - 2}$

Ines: *First I add $5 + 5$, and then add 2 more.*

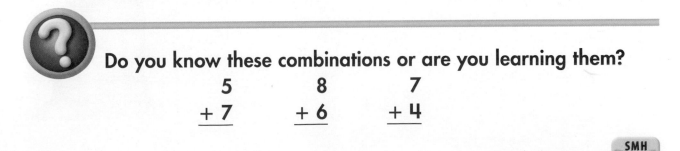

$$\underline{\quad 5 \quad} + \underline{\quad 7 \quad} =$$
$$\underline{\quad 7 \quad} + \underline{\quad 5 \quad} =$$

Clue: $\underline{5 + 5 + 2}$

? **Do you know these combinations or are you learning them?**

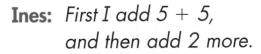

$$\begin{array}{r} 5 \\ + 7 \\ \hline \end{array} \qquad \begin{array}{r} 8 \\ + 6 \\ \hline \end{array} \qquad \begin{array}{r} 7 \\ + 4 \\ \hline \end{array}$$

Strategies for Solving Addition Problems (page 1 of 5)

There are different ways to solve addition problems.

Adding by Place

Gina used adding by place to solve this problem.

Bridget went to Sticker Station and bought 46 horse stickers and 74 space stickers. How many stickers did she buy altogether?

Gina's Solution

First I added the tens.	$40 + 70 = 110$
Then, I added the ones.	$6 + 4 = 10$
Then, I put the tens and ones together.	$110 + 10 = \mathbf{120}$

Gina's solution can also be shown using sticker sketches.

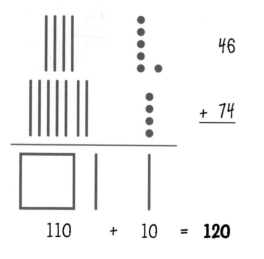

46

+ 74

110 + 10 = **120**

I traded 10 strips for a sheet and 10 singles for a strip, so I have 1 sheet and 2 strips.

Strategies for Solving Addition Problems (page 2 of 5)

Ines and Philip used adding by place when they solved this problem.

$$258$$
$$+\,392$$

They added the hundreds together, the tens together, and the ones together. Their solutions are similar, but they recorded their work differently.

Ines's Solution

$$200 + 300 = 500$$

$$50 + 90 = 140$$

$$8 + 2 = 10$$

$$500 + 140 + 10 = \mathbf{650}$$

Philip's Solution

$$258$$
$$+\,392$$
$$\overline{500}$$
$$140$$
$$+\,\underline{10}$$
$$\mathbf{650}$$

Ines recorded her solution sideways and Philip recorded his up and down.

? **How would you solve these problems?**

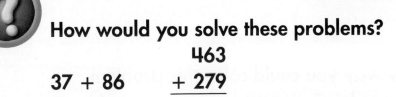

$$37 + 86 \qquad \begin{array}{r} 463 \\ +\,279 \\ \hline \end{array}$$

Strategies for Solving Addition Problems (page 3 of 5)

Adding One Number in Parts

Bridget went to Sticker Station and bought 46 horse stickers and 74 space stickers. How many stickers did she buy altogether?

Edwin solved the problem by starting at 74 on the number line and adding 46 in parts.

Edwin's Solution

$$46 = 20 + 20 + 6$$

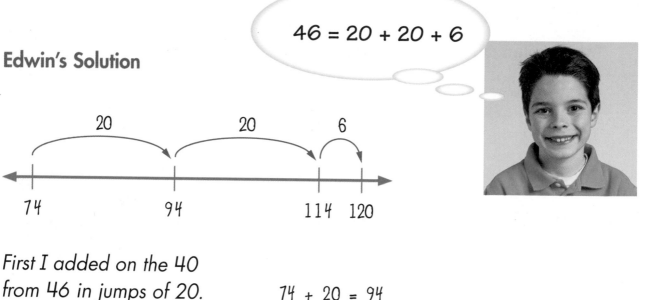

First I added on the 40 from 46 in jumps of 20.

$74 + 20 = 94$
$94 + 20 = 114$

Then I added the 6.

$114 + 6 = \textbf{120}$

Is there another way you could solve this problem by adding one number in parts?

Strategies for Solving Addition Problems (page 4 of 5)

258
+ 392   Kenji solved this problem by starting at 258 and adding 392 in parts.

Kenji's Solution

$$392 = 300 + 90 + 2$$

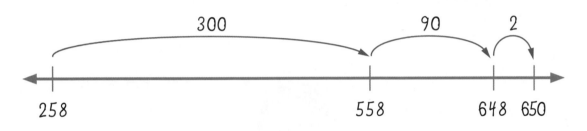

First I added the 300.   258 + 300 = 558
Then I added the 90.   558 + 90 = 648
Then I added the 2.   648 + 2 = **650**

Benjamin solved this problem by starting at 392 and adding 258 in parts.

Benjamin's Solution

$$258 = 8 + 250$$

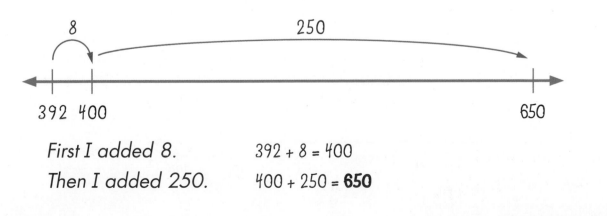

First I added 8.   392 + 8 = 400
Then I added 250.   400 + 250 = **650**

Strategies for Solving Addition Problems (page 5 of 5)

Changing the Numbers

Bridget went to Sticker Station and bought 46 horse stickers and 74 space stickers. How many stickers did she buy altogether?

Kathryn solved this problem by changing one number.

Kathryn's Solution

I added 4 to 46 to make 50. 50 is a "landmark" number, so it's easier for me to work with.

$46 + 4 = 50$

$$\begin{array}{r} 74 \\ +\ 50 \\ \hline 124 \\ -\ \ 4 \\ \hline \mathbf{120} \end{array}$$

I added 50 instead of 46.

Then I subtracted the extra 4.

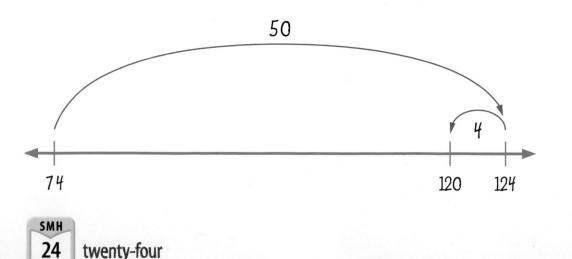

Adding More Than Two Numbers

Here is an addition problem with more than two numbers.

$$139 + 75 + 392$$

Denzel and Elena solved the problem in different ways.

Denzel solved the problem by breaking the numbers apart and adding by place.

Denzel's Solution

```
   139
    75
 + 392
```
   400   *I added the hundreds (100 + 300).*
   190   *I added the tens (30 + 70 + 90).*
 + 16   *I added the ones (9 + 5 + 2).*
   606   *Then I added up the parts to find the total.*

Elena solved the problem by changing the numbers to make an easier problem to solve.

Elena's Solution

131   400 *I took 8 from 139 and added it to 392.*
~~139~~ + 75 + ~~392~~ *That made the problem*
        8   131 + 75 + 400.

131 + 400 = 531   *I added the first number and the last number.*
531 + 5 = 536   *I added 75 in two parts.*
536 + 70 = **606**

How would you solve this problem?
139 + 75 + 392

Subtraction Situations

(page 1 of 3)

In Grade 3, you solve subtraction problems involving different types of subtraction situations.

One subtraction situation is *removing*. You solved many removal problems in Grade 2 and will solve more this year.

Removing an Amount

Gina had 165 famous people stickers. She sold 32 of them at a yard sale. How many stickers does Gina have left?

Here are the ways that some students solved this problem.

Elena solved this problem by drawing 165 stickers and crossing out 32 of them. The remaining stickers are the answer.

Elena's Solution

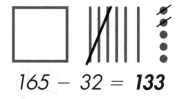

$$165 - 32 = \textbf{133}$$

Benjamin solved this problem by starting at 165 on the number line and subtracting back 32. The number he landed on is the answer.

Benjamin's Solution

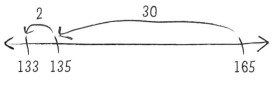

$$165 - 32 = \textbf{133}$$

? **How would you solve this problem?**

Subtraction Situations

(page 2 of 3)

In Grade 3, you also solve subtraction problems involving other types of subtraction situations—finding the unknown part and comparing.

Finding the Unknown Part of a Whole

Last week the Ruiz family drove to Loon Lake. Before leaving home, they set the trip meter of their car to 0. When they stopped for lunch at George's Restaurant, the trip meter read 87 miles. When they reached Loon Lake, the meter read 156 miles. How far did they travel from the restaurant to the lake?

In this subtraction problem, the unknown part is the distance from the restaurant to the lake.

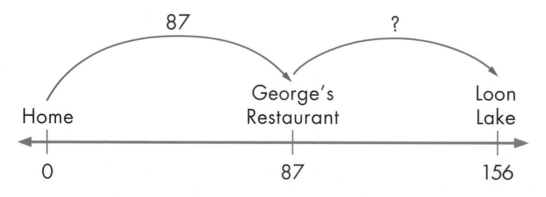

Subtraction Situations

(page 3 of 3)

Comparing Two Amounts

The rainbow snake at the nature center is 53 inches long. The boa constrictor is 84 inches long. How much longer is the boa constrictor?

In this subtraction problem, the lengths of two snakes are compared to find out how much longer one is than the other.

rainbow snake
53 inches long

boa constrictor
84 inches long

Tools to Represent Subtraction Problems (page 1 of 2)

On this page and the next, you will see some of the tools you can use to represent subtraction problems such as this one.

Ms. Santos's class is collecting cans for a recycling project. Their goal is to collect 175 cans. They have collected 63 cans so far. How many more cans do they need to collect to reach their goal?

$$63 + \underline{\ 112\ } = 175 \text{ or}$$
$$175 - 63 = \underline{\ 112\ }$$

Sticker Sketch

The answer is 112, the number of stickers that are left.

Number Line

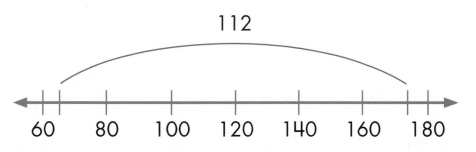

The answer is 112, the distance shown on the number line between the numbers 63 and 175.

Tools to Represent Subtraction Problems (page 2 of 2)

200 Chart

1	2	3	4	5	6	7	8	9	10
11	12	13	14	15	16	17	18	19	20
21	22	23	24	25	26	27	28	29	30
31	32	33	34	35	36	37	38	39	40
41	42	43	44	45	46	47	48	49	50
51	52	53	54	55	56	57	58	59	60
61	62	(63)	64	65	66	67	68	69	70
71	72	73	74	75	76	77	78	79	80
81	82	83	84	85	86	87	88	89	90
91	92	93	94	95	96	97	98	99	100
101	102	103	104	105	106	107	108	109	110
111	112	113	114	115	116	117	118	119	120
121	122	123	124	125	126	127	128	129	130
131	132	133	134	135	136	137	138	139	140
141	142	143	144	145	146	147	148	149	150
151	152	153	154	155	156	157	158	159	160
161	162	163	164	165	166	167	168	169	170
171	172	173	174	(175)	176	177	178	179	180
181	182	183	184	185	186	187	188	189	190
191	192	193	194	195	196	197	198	199	200

112

? Where in each representation on pages 29 and 30 do you see 175? Where in each representation do you see 63? Where in each representation do you see 112?

Subtraction Facts Related to Addition Combinations

One of your goals this year is to review and practice all of the addition combinations up to $10 + 10$. You can review strategies for practicing the addition combinations on pages 16–19.

Another goal is to learn the subtraction facts related to addition combinations.

Think of the addition combinations that you know when you solve related subtraction problems. Here are some examples.

$$6 + \underline{\textbf{4}} = 10$$

Think:
$10 - 6 = \underline{\textbf{4}}$

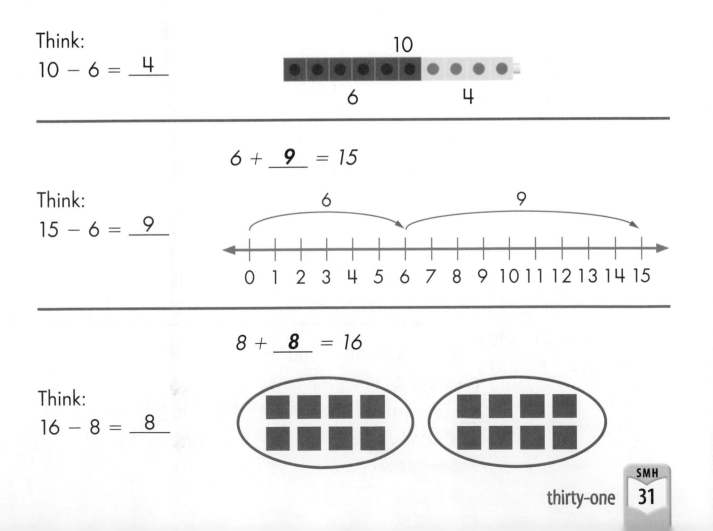

10

6   4

$$6 + \underline{\textbf{9}} = 15$$

Think:
$15 - 6 = \underline{\textbf{9}}$

$$8 + \underline{\textbf{8}} = 16$$

Think:
$16 - 8 = \underline{\textbf{8}}$

Strategies for Solving Subtraction Problems

(page 1 of 4)

Subtraction problems can be solved in different ways.

$$144 - 82 = \underline{\hphantom{xxxx}}$$

Adding Up

Bridget solved this problem by adding up. She started at 82 and added up to get to 144. She used 100 as a landmark number.

Bridget's Solution

$82 + \underline{\hphantom{xxxx}} = 144$

$82 + \underline{18} = 100$

$100 + \underline{44} = 144$

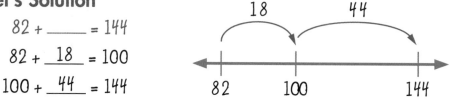

Bridget: *The answer is the total of the two jumps from 82 to 144.*
$18 + 44 =$ **62**

Subtracting Back

Keith solved the problem by subtracting back. He started at 144 and subtracted back to get to 82.

Keith's Solution

$144 - \underline{\hphantom{xxxx}} = 82$

$144 - \underline{4} = 140$

$140 - \underline{40} = 100$

$100 - \underline{10} = 90$

$90 - \underline{8} = 82$

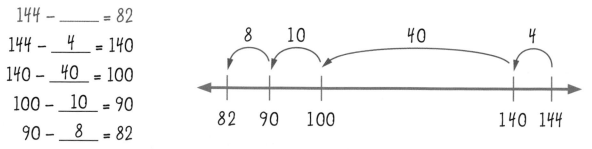

Keith: *The answer is the total of all the jumps from 144 back to 82.*
$4 + 40 + 10 + 8 =$ **62**

Strategies for Solving Subtraction Problems

(page 2 of 4)

This problem can be solved in different ways.

$$
\begin{array}{r}
924 \\
-\ 672 \\
\hline
\end{array}
$$

Adding Up

Jung solved this problem by starting at 672 and adding up to 924.

Jung's Solution

$672 +$ _____ $= 924$
$672 +$ _200_ $= 872$
$872 +$ _28_ $= 900$
$900 +$ _24_ $= 924$

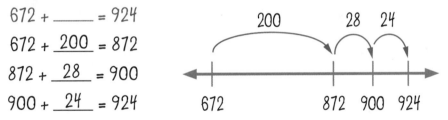

Jung: *The answer is the total of all the jumps from 672 up to 924.*
200 + 28 + 24 = **252**

Subtracting Back

Gil solved the problem by starting at 924 and subtracting back to 672.

Gil's Solution

$924 -$ _____ $= 672$
$924 -$ _24_ $= 900$
$900 -$ _200_ $= 700$
$700 -$ _28_ $= 672$

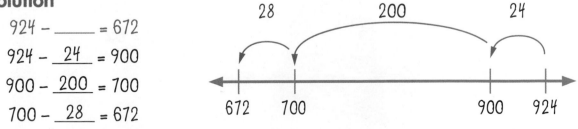

Gil: *The answer is the total of all the jumps from 924 back to 672.*
24 + 200 + 28 = **252**

Strategies for Solving Subtraction Problems

(page 3 of 4)

Subtracting One Number in Parts

$$144 - 82 = \underline{\qquad}$$

Kim solved this problem by starting with 144 and subtracting 82 in parts.

Kim's Solution

I started at 144 on the number line.

I subtracted 40 and landed on 104.   144 - 40 = 104

I subtracted 42 and landed on 62.   102 - 42 = 62

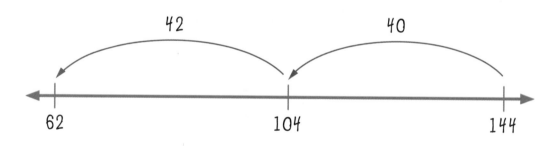

The answer is the number where I ended.
144 - 82 = **62**

Strategies for Solving Subtraction Problems

(page 4 of 4)

$$924$$
$$- 672$$

Arthur solved this problem by starting with 924 and subtracting 672 in parts.

Arthur's Solution

I started at 924.

I subtracted 600 and landed on 324.   924 – 600 = 324

I subtracted 20 and landed on 304.   324 – 20 = 304

I subtracted 50 and landed on 254.   304 – 50 = 254

Arthur: *Then I subtracted 2 and landed on 252.*   254 – 2 = 252

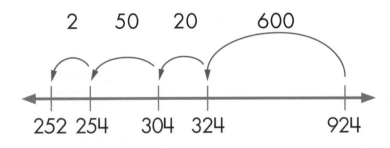

The answer is the number where I landed.   924 – 672 = **252**

How would you solve these problems?

Adding and Subtracting Tens and Hundreds

When you count by tens, you say the multiples of 10.

10, 20, 30, 40, 50, 60, 70, ...

What happens when you add a multiple of 10 to a number or subtract a multiple of 10 from a number?

Look at what these third-grade students noticed in these problems.

$$\begin{array}{r} 46 \\ + 30 \\ \hline 76 \end{array}$$

Dwayne:
46 has 4 tens. I added 30. The sum is 76, which has 7 tens because I added 3 more tens.

$$\begin{array}{r} 138 \\ - 30 \\ \hline 108 \end{array}$$

Pilar:
I start with 3 tens in the 38 part of 138. So if I subtract 3 tens, then all I have left is the 1 hundred and the 8 ones, so the answer is 108.

$$\begin{array}{r} 356 \\ + 200 \\ \hline 556 \end{array}$$

Beatriz:
356 has 3 hundreds. I added 200. The sum is 556, which has 5 hundreds because I added 2 more hundreds.

Solve these problems. Which digits change in the sums and differences?

565	565	565	565
+ 30	− 30	+ 300	− 300

Coin Values and Equivalencies (page 1 of 2)

Math Words
• **penny**
• **nickel**
• **dime**

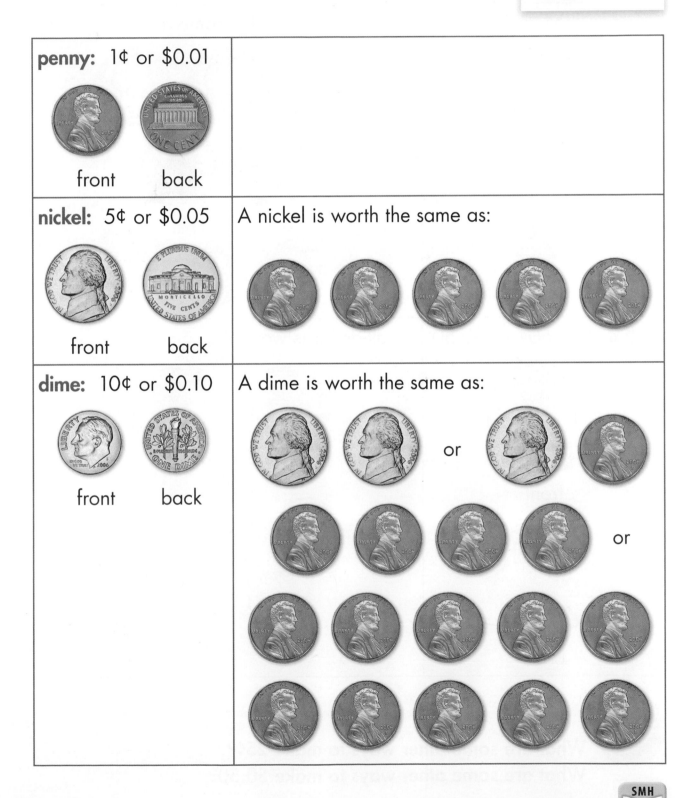

penny: 1¢ or $0.01

front   back

nickel: 5¢ or $0.05

front   back

A nickel is worth the same as:

dime: 10¢ or $0.10

front   back

A dime is worth the same as:

or

or

Coin Values and Equivalencies (page 2 of 2)

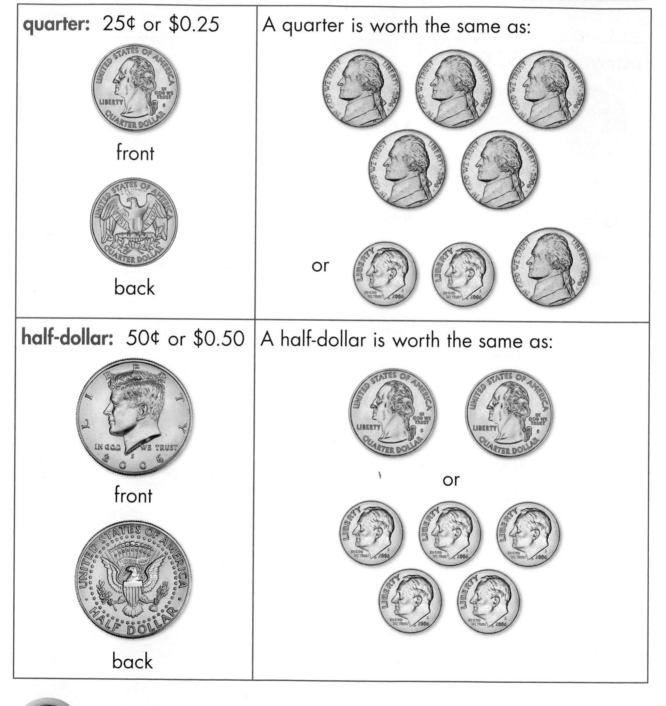

quarter: 25¢ or $0.25

front

back

A quarter is worth the same as:

or

half-dollar: 50¢ or $0.50

front

back

A half-dollar is worth the same as:

or

? What are some other ways to make 25¢?
What are some other ways to make $0.50?

Multiplication

Use multiplication when you want to combine groups that are the same size.

Math Words
- **multiplication**
- **factor**
- **product**

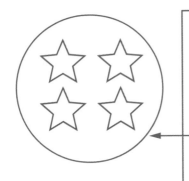

Here are 4 stars. ← **number of groups**

Each star has ← **number in each group**
5 points.

There are 20 points ← **number in all (product)**
in all.

$$4 \times 5 = 20$$

factors product

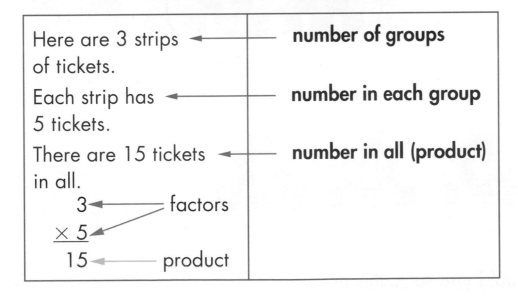

Here are 3 strips ← **number of groups**
of tickets.

Each strip has ← **number in each group**
5 tickets.

There are 15 tickets ← **number in all (product)**
in all.

$$
\begin{array}{r}
3 \\
\times\,5 \\
\hline
15
\end{array}
$$

factors

product

Solving Multiplication Problems (page 1 of 2)

How many cans are there?

Arthur used addition to solve this problem.

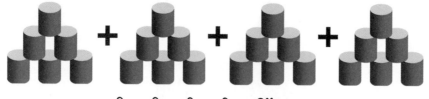

6 + 6 + 6 + 6 = **24** cans

Pilar used a multiplication combination she already knew.

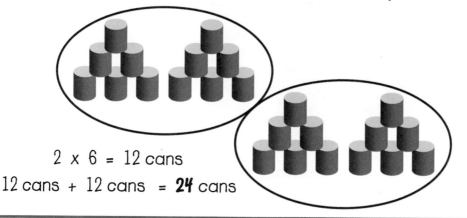

2 x 6 = 12 cans

12 cans + 12 cans = **24** cans

Kenji skip counted by 6s.

6, 12, 18, **24** cans

? **How would you solve this problem?**

Solving Multiplication Problems (page 2 of 2)

There are 5 hexagons.
There are 6 sides on each hexagon.
How many sides are there in all?

$5 \times 6 = $ ____

There are 4 flowers.
There are 5 petals on each flower.
How many petals are there in all?

$4 \times 5 = $ ____

There are 4 boxes of crayons.
There are 3 crayons in each box.
How many crayons are there in all?

$4 \times 3 = $ ____

 How would you solve these problems?

Skip Counting

Math Words
- skip counting
- multiples

This 100 chart shows skip counting by 3s.

The shaded numbers are multiples of 3.

1	2	3	4	5	6	7	8	9	10
11	12	13	14	15	16	17	18	19	20
21	22	23	24	25	26	27	28	29	30
31	32	33	34	35	36	37	38	39	40
41	42	43	44	45	46	47	48	49	50
51	52	53	54	55	56	57	58	59	60
61	62	63	64	65	66	67	68	69	70
71	72	73	74	75	76	77	78	79	80
81	82	83	84	85	86	87	88	89	90
91	92	93	94	95	96	97	98	99	100

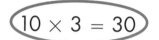

$10 \times 3 = 30$

Cubes stacked in groups of 3 also show skip counting by 3s.

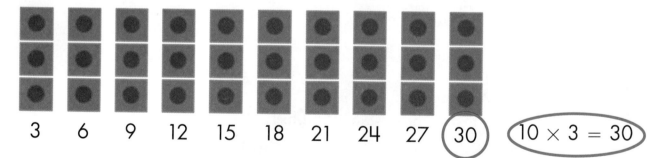

3   6   9   12   15   18   21   24   27   30 $10 \times 3 = 30$

A number line can also show skip counting.

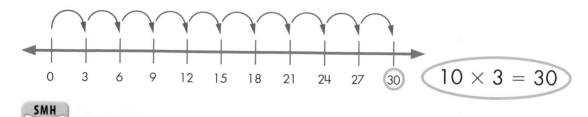

$10 \times 3 = 30$

Multiples of 5 and Multiples of 10

Some students found the multiples of 5 and 10 on these 100 charts.

Multiples of 5									
1	2	3	4	5	6	7	8	9	10
11	12	13	14	15	16	17	18	19	20
21	22	23	24	25	26	27	28	29	30
31	32	33	34	35	36	37	38	39	40
41	42	43	44	45	46	47	48	49	50
51	52	53	54	55	56	57	58	59	60
61	62	63	64	65	66	67	68	69	70
71	72	73	74	75	76	77	78	79	80
81	82	83	84	85	86	87	88	89	90
91	92	93	94	95	96	97	98	99	100

Multiples of 10									
1	2	3	4	5	6	7	8	9	10
11	12	13	14	15	16	17	18	19	20
21	22	23	24	25	26	27	28	29	30
31	32	33	34	35	36	37	38	39	40
41	42	43	44	45	46	47	48	49	50
51	52	53	54	55	56	57	58	59	60
61	62	63	64	65	66	67	68	69	70
71	72	73	74	75	76	77	78	79	80
81	82	83	84	85	86	87	88	89	90
91	92	93	94	95	96	97	98	99	100

Here are some of the things they noticed.

- *All of the multiples of 10 are even numbers. The multiples of 5 go odd, even, odd, even.*
- *There are twice as many multiples of 5 on the 100 chart as there are multiples of 10.*
- *The multiples of 10 are all in the last column of the 100 chart. The multiples of 5 are in two columns.*

What else do you notice about the multiples of 5 and 10?

Solving Related Multiplication Problems

Here are two related problems.

Cats have 4 legs.
How many legs are on 5 cats?
How many legs are on 8 cats?

Ines solved both problems. She used the answer to the first problem to help her figure out the answer to the second problem.

How many legs are on 5 cats?

5 cats
IIII IIII IIII IIII IIII
20 legs
$5 \times 4 = 20$

How many legs are on 8 cats?

5 cats	3 cats
IIII IIII IIII IIII IIII	IIII IIII IIII
20 legs	12 legs
$5 \times 4 = 20$	$3 \times 4 = 12$

5 cats + 3 cats = 8 cats
IIII IIII IIII IIII IIII + IIII IIII IIII
20 legs + 12 legs = 32 legs
$8 \times 4 = 32$

How would you solve these related problems?
Spiders have 8 legs.
- **How many legs are on 3 spiders?**
- **How many legs are on 6 spiders?**

Arrays

Here is an array of chairs.

Math Words
- array
- dimension
- factor

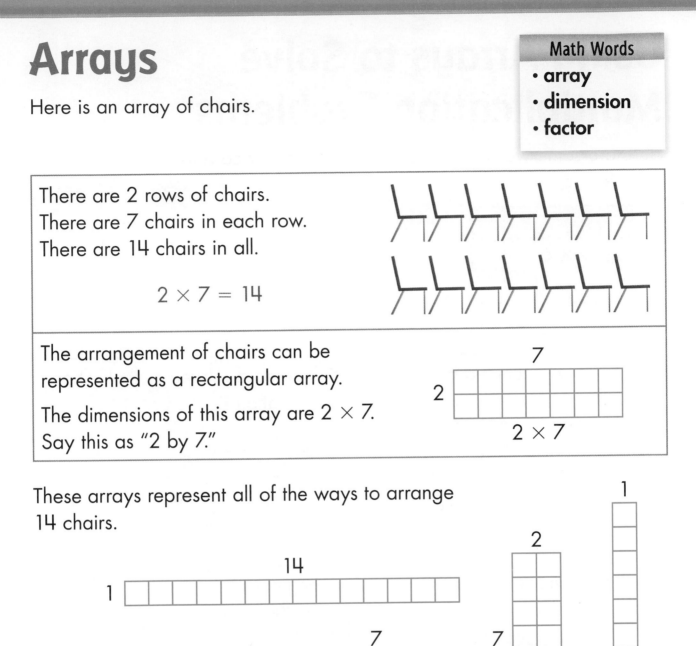

There are 2 rows of chairs.
There are 7 chairs in each row.
There are 14 chairs in all.

$$2 \times 7 = 14$$

The arrangement of chairs can be represented as a rectangular array.

The dimensions of this array are 2 × 7.
Say this as "2 by 7."

7
2
2×7

These arrays represent all of the ways to arrange 14 chairs.

14
1

Dimensions: 1 by 14
2 by 7
7 by 2
14 by 1

7
2

2
7

1
2
7
14

The numbers 1, 2, 7, and 14 are factors of 14.

? **Find all the arrays for 16.**

Using Arrays to Solve Multiplication Problems

Here are some ways that students used an array card to solve 4 × 6.

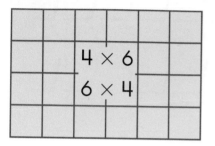

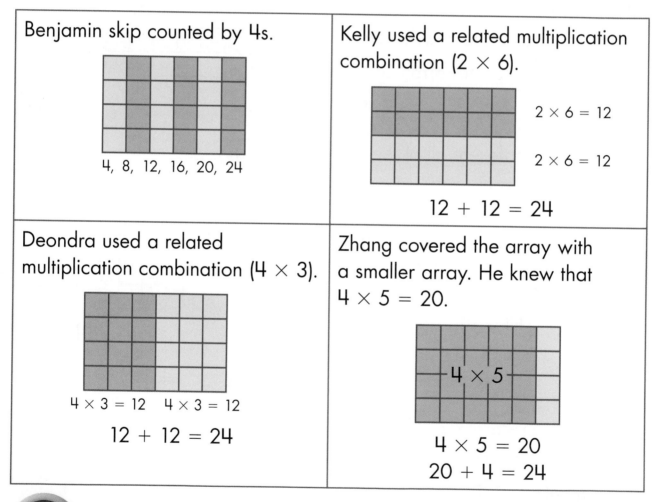

Benjamin skip counted by 4s.

4, 8, 12, 16, 20, 24

Kelly used a related multiplication combination (2 × 6).

2 × 6 = 12

2 × 6 = 12

12 + 12 = 24

Deondra used a related multiplication combination (4 × 3).

4 × 3 = 12   4 × 3 = 12

12 + 12 = 24

Zhang covered the array with a smaller array. He knew that 4 × 5 = 20.

4 × 5 = 20

20 + 4 = 24

How would you solve this problem?

Division

Use division when you want to separate a quantity into equal-sized groups.

number in all ⟶ Here are 20 balloons.
number of groups ⟶ There are 5 friends.
number in each group ⟶ Each friend has 4 balloons.

$$20 \div 5 = 4$$

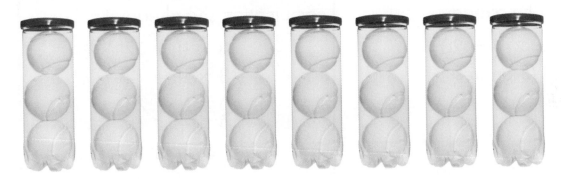

number in all ⟶ Here are 24 tennis balls.
number of groups ⟶ There are 8 cans of tennis balls.
number in each group ⟶ Each can holds 3 tennis balls.

$$3\overline{)24}$$ with 8 above.

Solving Division Problems

Oscar has 24 marbles. He wants to put 4 marbles in a bag. How many bags can Oscar fill?

$24 \div 4 =$ _____ $4\overline{)24}$ _____ $\times 4 = 24$

Here are the ways that some students solved this problem.

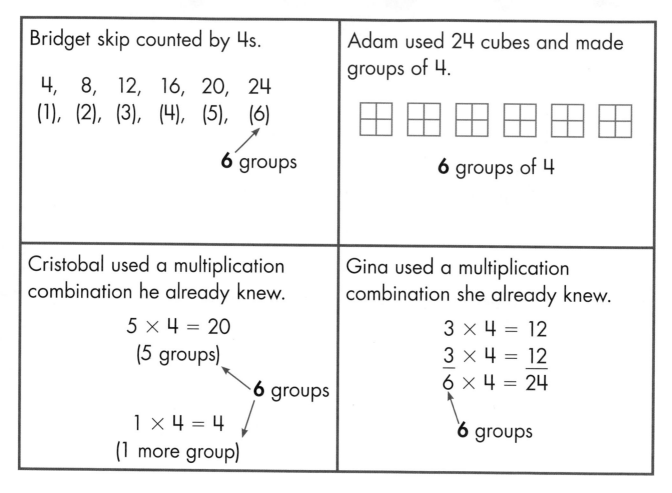

Bridget skip counted by 4s.

4,   8,   12,   16,   20,   24
(1),   (2),   (3),   (4),   (5),   (6)

6 groups

Adam used 24 cubes and made groups of 4.

6 groups of 4

Cristobal used a multiplication combination he already knew.

$5 \times 4 = 20$
(5 groups)

6 groups

$1 \times 4 = 4$
(1 more group)

Gina used a multiplication combination she already knew.

$3 \times 4 = 12$
$\dfrac{3 \times 4 = 12}{6 \times 4 = 24}$

6 groups

Oscar can fill **6** bags.

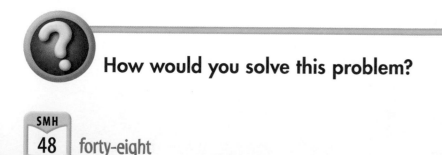

? **How would you solve this problem?**

Multiplication Combinations (page 1 of 3)

Here are some ways to help you learn the multiplication combinations with products up to 50.

Learning Two Combinations at a Time

5×3 and 3×5

These two problems look different, but they have the same answer.

When you know that $5 \times 3 = 15$, you also know that $3 \times 5 = 15$.

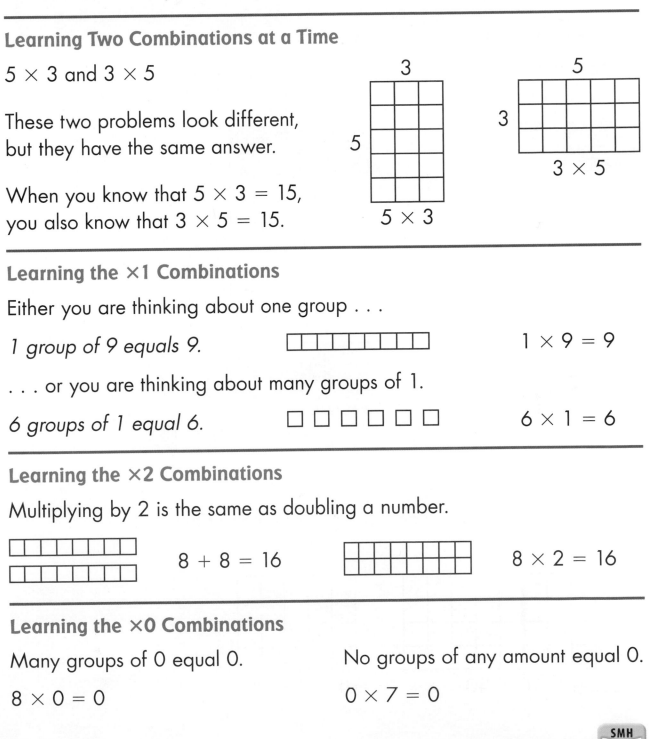

Learning the ×1 Combinations

Either you are thinking about one group . . .

1 group of 9 equals 9. $1 \times 9 = 9$

. . . or you are thinking about many groups of 1.

6 groups of 1 equal 6. $6 \times 1 = 6$

Learning the ×2 Combinations

Multiplying by 2 is the same as doubling a number.

$8 + 8 = 16$ $8 \times 2 = 16$

Learning the ×0 Combinations

Many groups of 0 equal 0.   No groups of any amount equal 0.

$8 \times 0 = 0$ $0 \times 7 = 0$

Multiplication Combinations (page 2 of 3)

Here are more ways to help you learn multiplication combinations.

Double a Combination You Know

To learn the ×4 combinations, you can double the ×2 combinations.

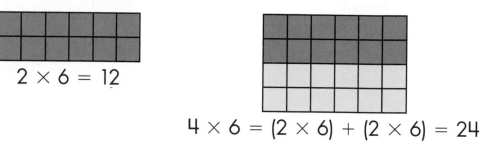

$2 \times 6 = 12$

$4 \times 6 = (2 \times 6) + (2 \times 6) = 24$

To learn the ×6 combinations, you can double the ×3 combinations.

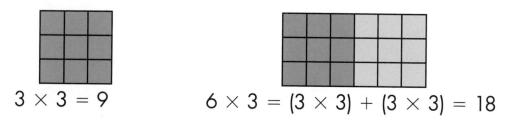

$3 \times 3 = 9$

$6 \times 3 = (3 \times 3) + (3 \times 3) = 18$

Take Half of a Combination You Know

To learn the ×5 combinations, you can take half of the ×10 combinations.

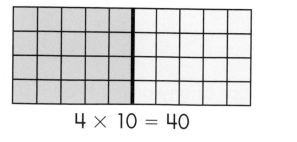

$4 \times 10 = 40$

$4 \times 5 = 20$

Multiplication Combinations (page 3 of 3)

As you practice the multiplication combinations, make lists of the ones you "just know" and the ones that you are "working on" learning.

	"Combinations I Know"	"Combinations I'm Working On"

One way to practice a combination you're working on is to make a Multiplication Clue Card. Think of a combination you already know that you can start with to help you learn the harder one.

Here are the ways two students solved 4×8. Each student used a different strategy.

Noemi started with 4×4. Then she doubled it.

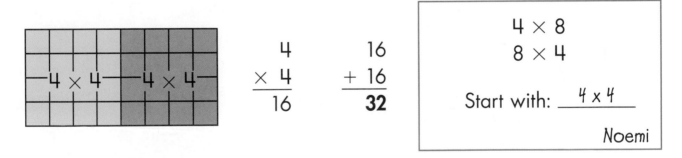

$$\begin{array}{r} 4 \\ \times\ 4 \\ \hline 16 \end{array} \qquad \begin{array}{r} 16 \\ +\ 16 \\ \hline \mathbf{32} \end{array}$$

> 4×8
> 8×4
>
> Start with: ___4 x 4___
>
> Noemi

Gil started with 4×5. Then he added 4×3.

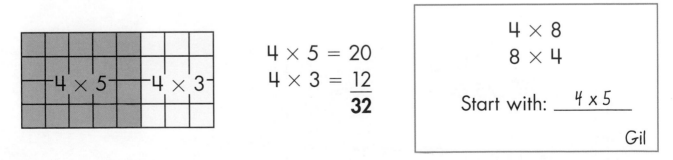

$$\begin{array}{l} 4 \times 5 = 20 \\ 4 \times 3 = \underline{12} \\ \ \mathbf{32} \end{array}$$

> 4×8
> 8×4
>
> Start with: ___4 x 5___
>
> Gil

Square Numbers

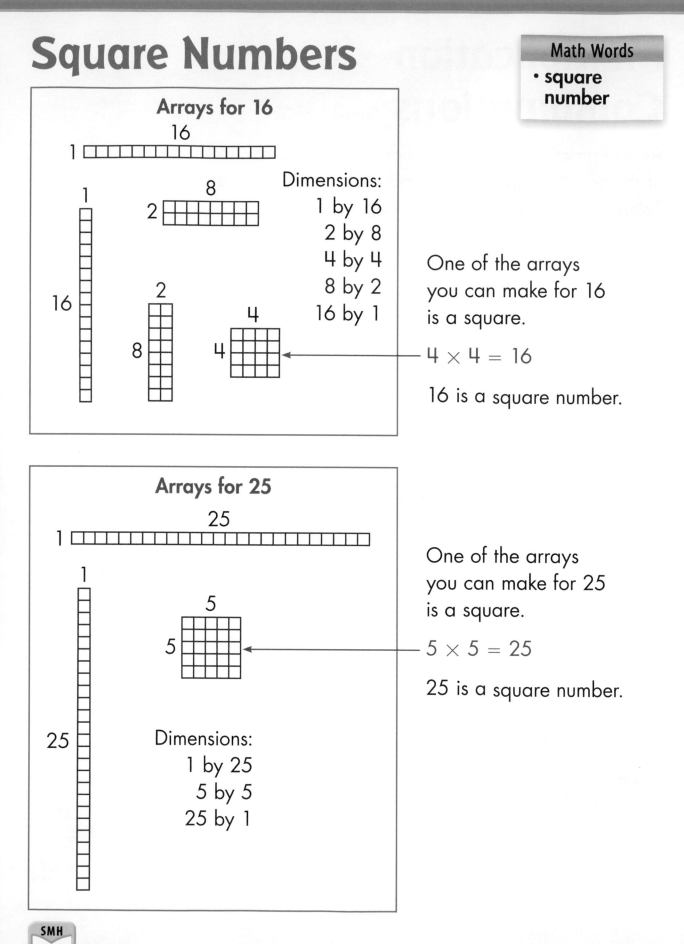

Arrays for 16

16

1

8
2

1

16

2

8

4
4

Dimensions:
1 by 16
2 by 8
4 by 4
8 by 2
16 by 1

One of the arrays you can make for 16 is a square.

$4 \times 4 = 16$

16 is a square number.

Arrays for 25

25

1

1

25

5
5

Dimensions:
1 by 25
5 by 5
25 by 1

One of the arrays you can make for 25 is a square.

$5 \times 5 = 25$

25 is a square number.

Prime Numbers

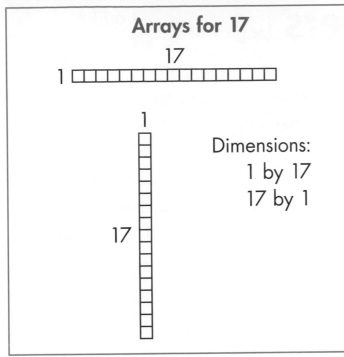

Arrays for 17

Dimensions:
1 by 17
17 by 1

You can make only two arrays for 17.

$17 \times 1 = 17$
$1 \times 17 = 17$

The only factors of 17 are 17 and 1.

17 is a prime number.

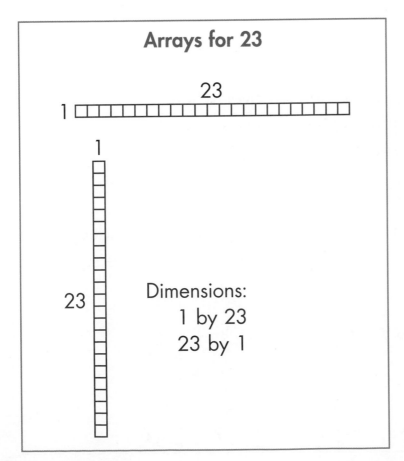

Arrays for 23

Dimensions:
1 by 23
23 by 1

You can make only two arrays for 23.

$23 \times 1 = 23$
$1 \times 23 = 23$

The only factors of 23 are 23 and 1.

23 is a prime number.

Even Numbers and Odd Numbers (page 1 of 2)

An even number of things can be divided into groups of 2 without any leftovers. An even number of things can be divided into two equal groups of whole things.

10 is an even number.

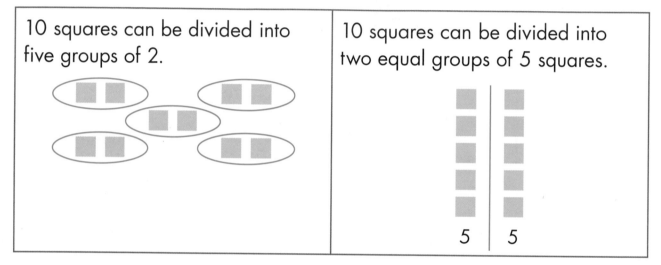

10 squares can be divided into five groups of 2.	10 squares can be divided into two equal groups of 5 squares.

An odd number of things always has one left over when divided into groups of 2. An odd number of things cannot be divided into two equal groups of whole things.

13 is an odd number.

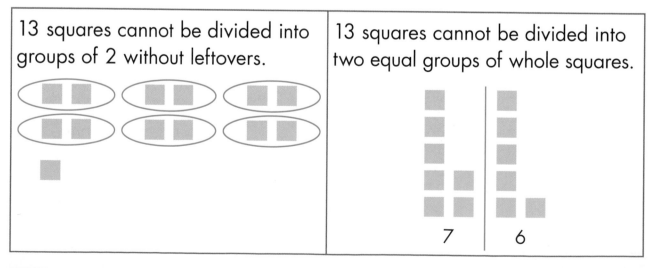

13 squares cannot be divided into groups of 2 without leftovers.	13 squares cannot be divided into two equal groups of whole squares.

Even Numbers and Odd Numbers (page 2 of 2)

This 100 chart shows skip counting by 2s.

1	2	3	4	5	6	7	8	9	10
11	12	13	14	15	16	17	18	19	20
21	22	23	24	25	26	27	28	29	30
31	32	33	34	35	36	37	38	39	40
41	42	43	44	45	46	47	48	49	50
51	52	53	54	55	56	57	58	59	60
61	62	63	64	65	66	67	68	69	70
71	72	73	74	75	76	77	78	79	80
81	82	83	84	85	86	87	88	89	90
91	92	93	94	95	96	97	98	99	100

If you start at 0 and count by 2s, you will say even numbers. The even numbers on this chart are yellow.

If you start at 1 and count by 2s, you will say odd numbers. The odd numbers on this chart are white.

Is 43 even or odd?
Is 70 even or odd?
Is 101 even or odd?

Fractions

Math Words
• **fraction**

Fractions are numbers.

Some fractions, such as $\frac{1}{4}$ and $\frac{1}{2}$, are less than 1.

Some fractions, such as $\frac{2}{2}$ and $\frac{4}{4}$, are equal to 1.

Some fractions, such as $\frac{6}{4}$ and $\frac{3}{2}$, are greater than 1.

Fractions can be used to show parts of a whole.

One third of this flag is white.

The whole flag has 3 equal parts, or stripes. $\searrow$ $\frac{1}{3}$ $\leftarrow$ One stripe is white.

1 out of the 3 equal parts is white.

Three fourths of these balloons are red.

There are 4 balloons in the whole group. $\searrow$ $\frac{3}{4}$ $\leftarrow$ Three of the balloons are red.

3 out of 4 equal parts are red.

? **What fraction of the flag is blue?**
What fraction of the balloons is yellow?

Fractions of an Area

Nancy, Murphy, Kelly, and Adam have one brownie to share equally.

Nancy cut the brownie into four pieces. All of the pieces are the same size.

Each person gets $\frac{1}{4}$ of the brownie.

Nancy ← | → Kelly

Murphy ← | → Adam

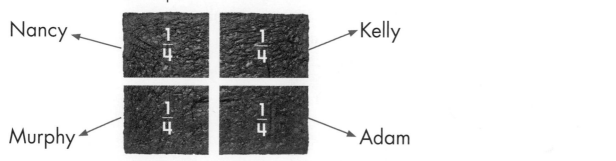

Fraction Notation:

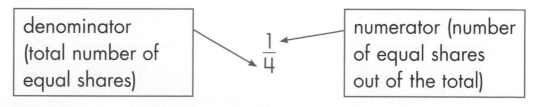

denominator (total number of equal shares) $\frac{1}{4}$ numerator (number of equal shares out of the total)

Here are some other ways to cut one brownie into fourths.

 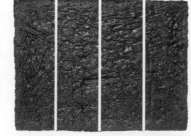

Naming Fractions (page 1 of 2)

In each of these examples, one whole rectangle has been divided into equal parts. The part of the rectangle shaded blue and the part of the rectangle shaded yellow are named.

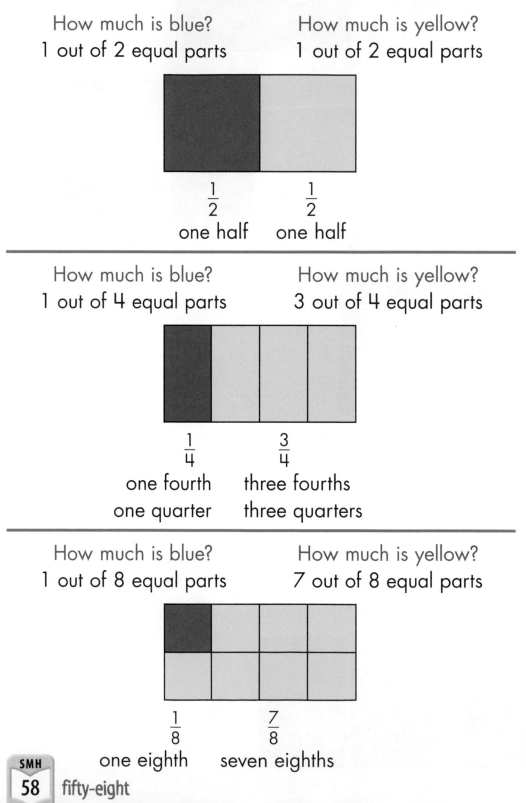

How much is blue?
1 out of 2 equal parts

How much is yellow?
1 out of 2 equal parts

$\frac{1}{2}$ $\frac{1}{2}$
one half   one half

How much is blue?
1 out of 4 equal parts

How much is yellow?
3 out of 4 equal parts

$\frac{1}{4}$ $\frac{3}{4}$
one fourth   three fourths
one quarter   three quarters

How much is blue?
1 out of 8 equal parts

How much is yellow?
7 out of 8 equal parts

$\frac{1}{8}$ $\frac{7}{8}$
one eighth   seven eighths

Naming Fractions (page 2 of 2)

How much is blue?
1 out of 3 equal parts

How much is yellow?
2 out of 3 equal parts

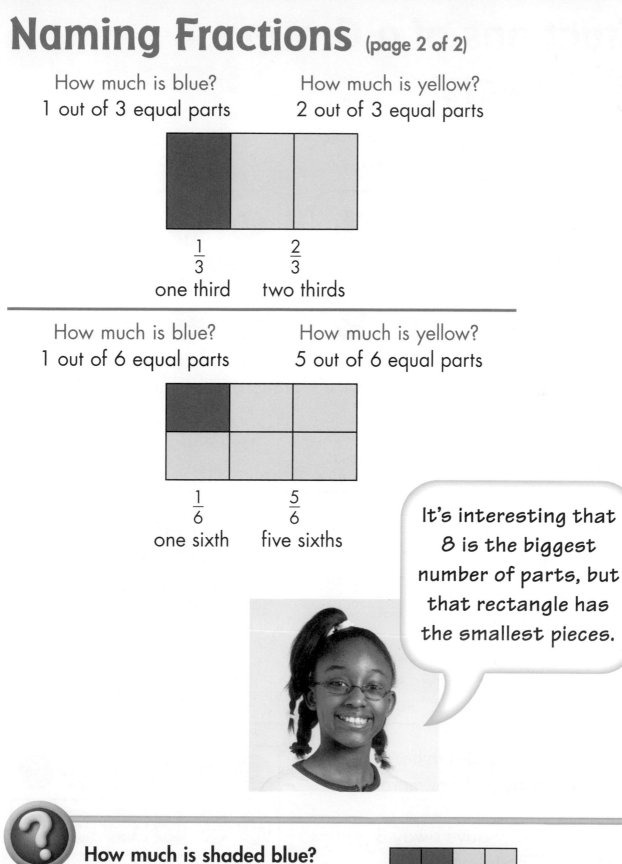

$\frac{1}{3}$ $\frac{2}{3}$

one third   two thirds

How much is blue?
1 out of 6 equal parts

How much is yellow?
5 out of 6 equal parts

$\frac{1}{6}$ $\frac{5}{6}$

one sixth   five sixths

It's interesting that 8 is the biggest number of parts, but that rectangle has the smallest pieces.

How much is shaded blue?
How much is shaded yellow?

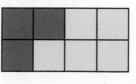

Fractions of a Group of Objects

Three people share 15 apples equally.
Each person gets $\frac{1}{3}$ of the apples.

3 equal groups ⟶ $\dfrac{1}{3}$ ⟶ 1 group for each person

$\frac{1}{3}$ of 15 is **5.**

There are 64 squares on a checkers board. Half of them are red.

$\dfrac{1}{2}$ ⟶ 1 group is red
⟶ 2 equal groups

$\frac{1}{2}$ of 64 is **32.**

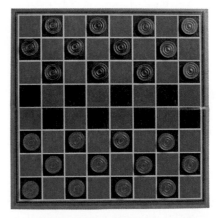

Becky had 12 marbles in her collections. She gave away $\frac{3}{4}$ of her marbles.

$\dfrac{3}{4}$ ⟶ Becky gave away 3 groups.
⟶ 4 equal groups

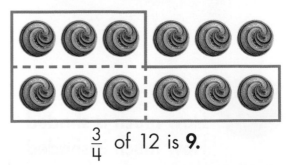

$\frac{3}{4}$ of 12 is **9.**

Using Fractions for Quantities Greater Than One (page 1 of 2)

Math Words
• mixed number

Edwin and Pilar solved a problem about people and brownies. Each person's share is greater than one.

Two people shared 3 brownies equally. How much does each person get?

Edwin's Solution:

First I gave one whole brownie to each person.

There was one brownie left. I split it into 2 equal pieces and gave each person one-half.

Each person gets $1\frac{1}{2}$.

A mixed number has a whole number part and a fractional part.

whole number →$1\frac{1}{2}$← fraction

one and one-half

Using Fractions for Quantities Greater Than One (page 2 of 2)

Pilar's Solution:

I cut all the brownies into 2 equal pieces. Each person gets 1 piece, or half, of each brownie.

Each person gets $\frac{3}{2}$.

$\frac{1}{2} + \frac{1}{2} + \frac{1}{2} = \frac{3}{2}$

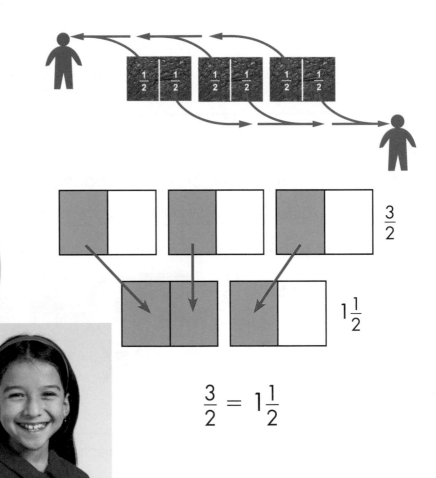

$$\frac{3}{2} = 1\frac{1}{2}$$

My answer is really just the same as Edwin's answer. Two halves from the three halves is one whole. Then there is one more half.

? If 3 people shared 4 brownies equally, how much would each person get?

If 3 people shared 5 brownies equally, how much would each person get?

Equivalent Fractions

Math Words
- **equivalent fractions**

Different fractions that name the same amount are called equivalent fractions.

Keith used pattern blocks to show some equivalent fractions.

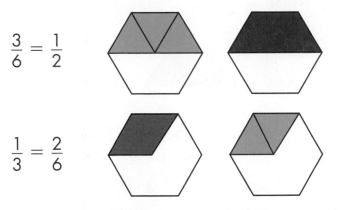

$$\frac{3}{6} = \frac{1}{2}$$

$$\frac{1}{3} = \frac{2}{6}$$

Jane showed some other equivalent fractions by using rectangles.

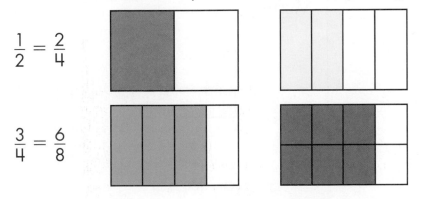

$$\frac{1}{2} = \frac{2}{4}$$

$$\frac{3}{4} = \frac{6}{8}$$

Chris showed that $\frac{1}{2}$ and $\frac{4}{8}$ are equivalent fractions by using a group of 8 cubes.

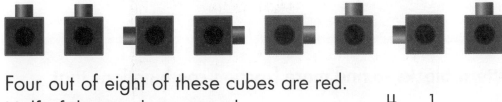

Four out of eight of these cubes are red.
Half of these cubes are red.

$$\frac{4}{8} = \frac{1}{2}$$

What two equivalent fractions name the portion of red cubes?

Fraction Combinations

These students wrote equations to show the fraction parts and totals for each of these pictures.

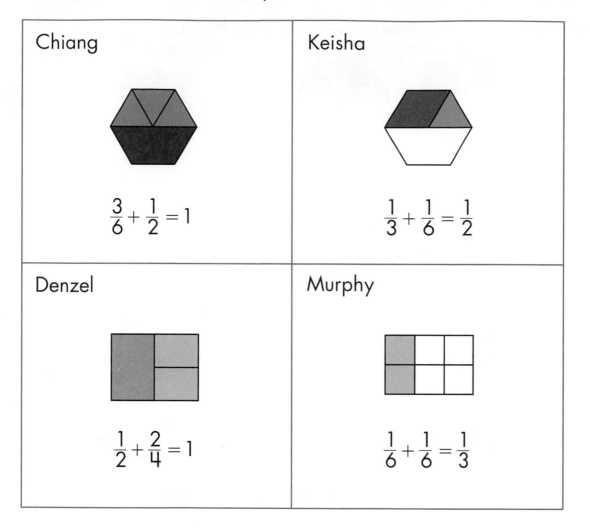

Chiang

$$\frac{3}{6} + \frac{1}{2} = 1$$

Keisha

$$\frac{1}{3} + \frac{1}{6} = \frac{1}{2}$$

Denzel

$$\frac{1}{2} + \frac{2}{4} = 1$$

Murphy

$$\frac{1}{6} + \frac{1}{6} = \frac{1}{3}$$

Use pattern blocks to find more fraction combinations that equal 1.

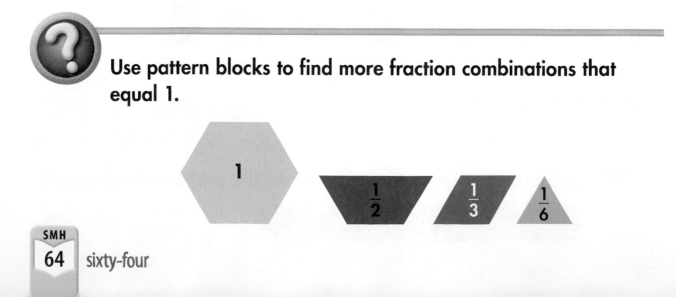

Fractions and Decimals That Are Equal

Math Words
- **decimal**
- **decimal point**

Numbers that include decimal points are called decimals.
Some numbers can be written as either fractions or decimals.

These problems can be answered by using fractions or decimals.

Four people share one dollar equally. How much money does each person get?

Fraction answer:
Each person gets $\frac{1}{4}$ dollar.

Decimal answer:
Each person gets $0.25.

$$\frac{1}{4} = 0.25$$

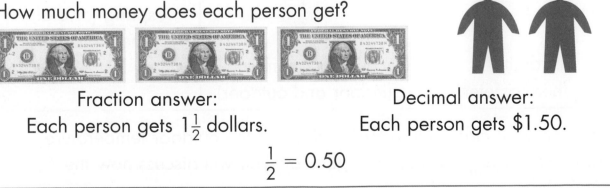

Two people share three dollars equally.
How much money does each person get?

Fraction answer:
Each person gets $1\frac{1}{2}$ dollars.

Decimal answer:
Each person gets $1.50.

$$\frac{1}{2} = 0.50$$

What's the Temperature?

(page 1 of 4)

Math Words
- **Celsius**
- **degree**
- **Fahrenheit**

How warm or cold is it outside? You can find out by using a thermometer to measure the temperature.

Temperature is measured in two different scales: degrees Fahrenheit and degrees Celsius.

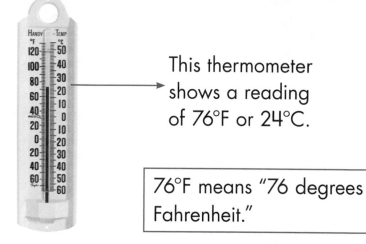

This thermometer shows a reading of 76°F or 24°C.

76°F means "76 degrees Fahrenheit."

Thermometers in many styles are used to measure outdoor temperature.

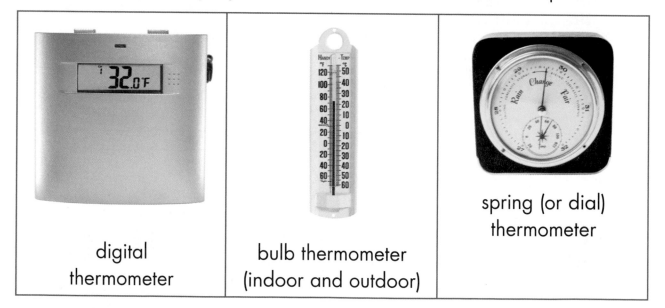

digital thermometer

bulb thermometer (indoor and outdoor)

spring (or dial) thermometer

This year, your class will record and graph the outdoor temperature every Wednesday. As the year goes by, you will discuss how the temperature changes in your area.

What's the Temperature?

(page 2 of 4)

This map shows the temperature in degrees Fahrenheit across the United States for a day in September.

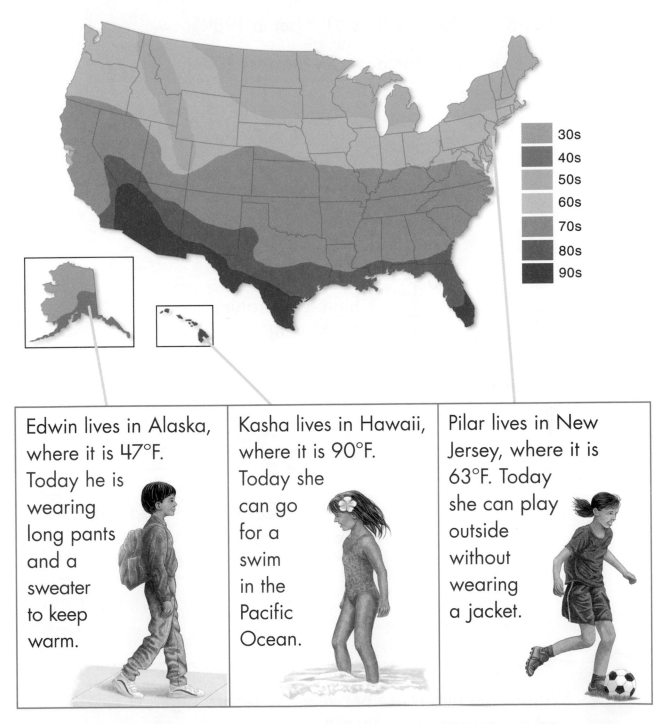

30s
40s
50s
60s
70s
80s
90s

Edwin lives in Alaska, where it is 47°F. Today he is wearing long pants and a sweater to keep warm.

Kasha lives in Hawaii, where it is 90°F. Today she can go for a swim in the Pacific Ocean.

Pilar lives in New Jersey, where it is 63°F. Today she can play outside without wearing a jacket.

What's the Temperature?

(page 3 of 4)

The average temperature in Anchorage, Alaska for the month of March is 26°F.

The record high for March is 51°F (set in 1984).

The record low for March is −24°F (set in 1971).

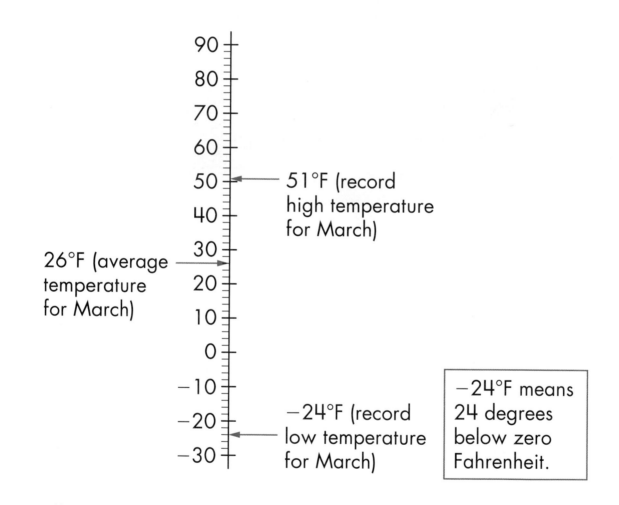

26°F (average temperature for March)

51°F (record high temperature for March)

−24°F (record low temperature for March)

−24°F means 24 degrees below zero Fahrenheit.

What is the difference between the record high (51°F) and the record low (−24°F)?

What's the Temperature?

(page 4 of 4)

Here is the temperature graph from Keith's class at the end of September.

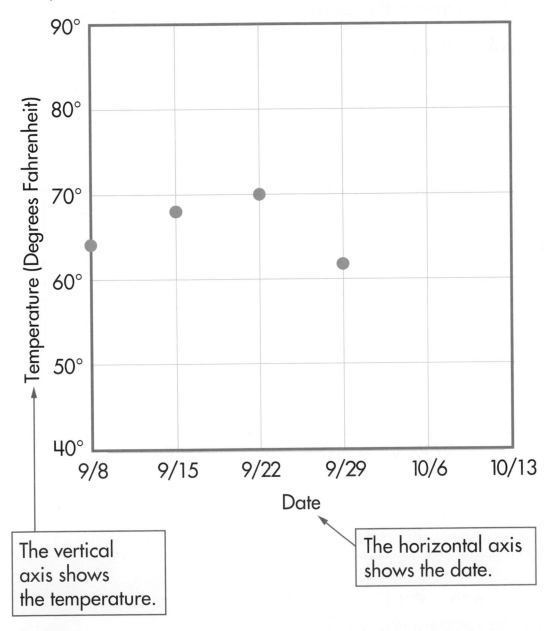

The vertical axis shows the temperature.

The horizontal axis shows the date.

? **What state might Keith live in?**

Reading Points on a Line Graph

Each point on this graph represents two connected pieces of information, the date and the temperature.

For example, look at the point marked with a star (☆) on the graph.

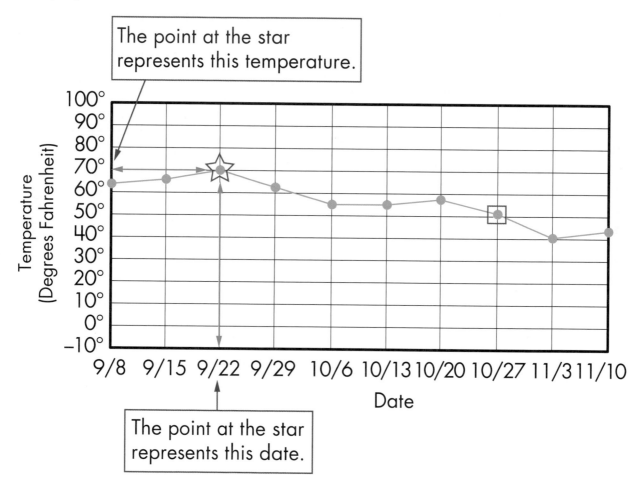

The point at the star represents this temperature.

The point at the star represents this date.

The point marked with a star (☆) shows that on September 22 the temperature was 70°F.

What does the point marked with a square (☐) tell you?

Telling Stories from Line Graphs (page 1 of 2)

Each of these line graphs represents part of a temperature graph.

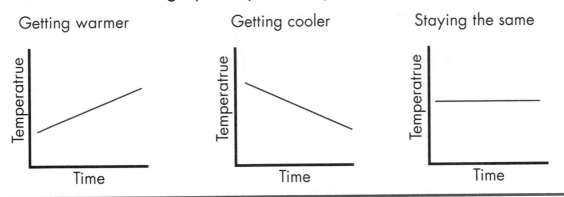

Getting warmer

Getting cooler

Staying the same

Here is a complete temperature graph for one spring day.

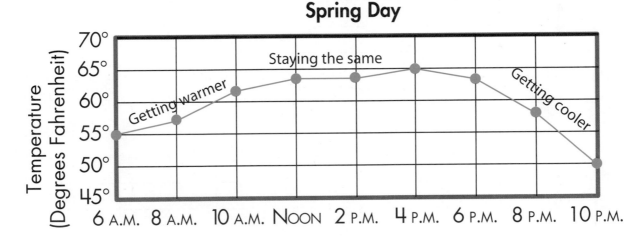

Spring Day

Kathryn wrote this story about the weather on the spring day represented on the graph.

When I woke up it was cloudy and cool. By noon the sun came out and it was warm enough to play outside. In the evening it got cooler and I needed an extra blanket to sleep that night.

What is the highest temperature? What is the lowest temperature? What is the difference between the highest and lowest temperatures?

Telling Stories from Line Graphs (page 2 of 2)

This line graph shows how the temperature changed in Anchorage, Alaska over time from January to June.

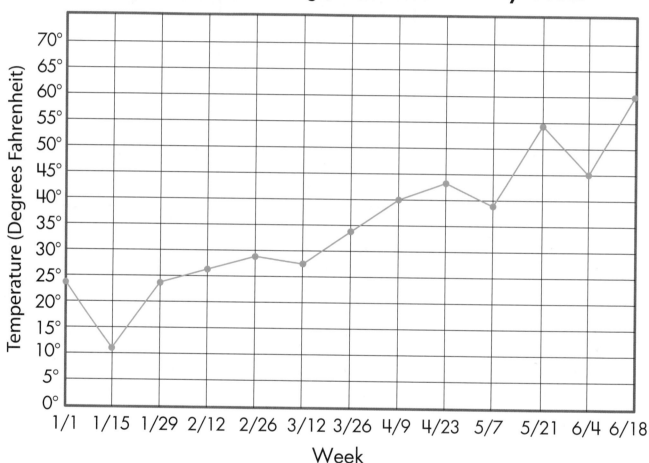

Temperature in Anchorage, Alaska from January to June

Look at the overall shape of the graph.
In general, what is happening to the temperature in Anchorage from January to June? Is it getting warmer?
Is it getting cooler? Is it staying the same?
What else do you notice?

Repeating Patterns

(page 1 of 2)

Math Words
• unit

Here are some repeating patterns made with connecting cubes.

The unit is the part of the pattern that repeats over and over.

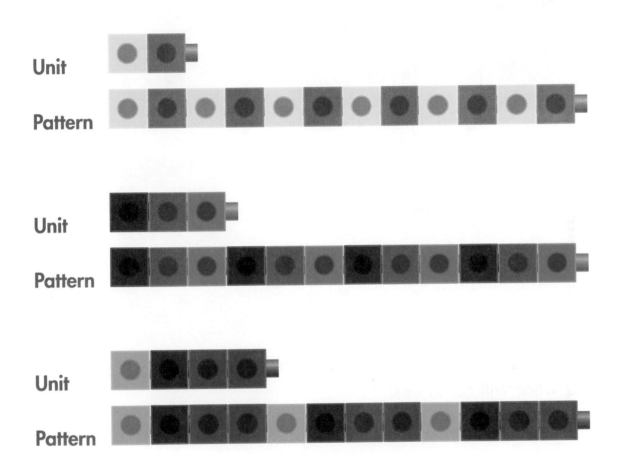

What is the unit in this repeating pattern?

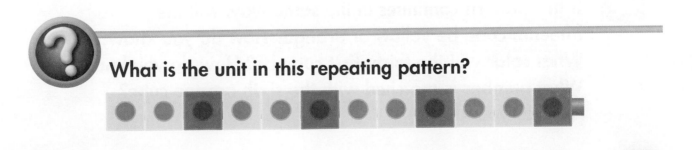

Repeating Patterns (page 2 of 2)

In this repeating pattern, each cube is numbered.

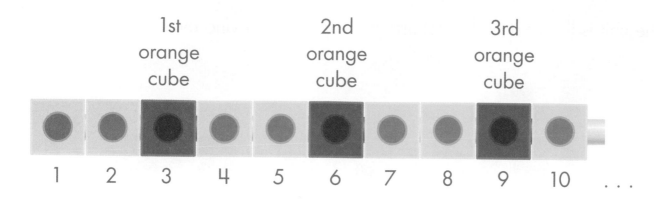

1st orange cube   2nd orange cube   3rd orange cube

1   2   3   4   5   6   7   8   9   10   . . .

In this pattern the first orange cube is cube 3.

The second orange cube is cube 6.

The third orange cube is cube 9.

When a pattern repeats, you can use what you know to figure out what will come next.

?

If this pattern continues in the same way, will the fifteenth cube be yellow or orange? How do you know? What color will the thirty-first cube be? How do you know? What number is matched with the sixth orange cube? How do you know?

The Magic Marbles of Rhomaar (page 1 of 6)

A Situation of Constant Change

On the planet Rhomaar, children receive Magic Marbles as gifts. The children on Rhomaar can use these Magic Marbles to buy toys, books, snacks, and other things they like.

For the first 30 nights of each year, each child on Rhomaar is visited by a Magic Marble Messenger, who leaves that child the same number of Magic Marbles each night. On the first night of the year, the children find out how many marbles they will receive each night for 30 nights. This number can be different for different Rhomaarian children.

The Magic Marbles are so valuable that many children do not use all their Magic Marbles in any one year and may save some for the next year. So every year, some children start with leftover marbles and some do not.

The Magic Marbles of Rhomaar (page 2 of 6)

A Situation of Constant Change, *continued*

Leeyan lives on the planet Rhomaar. She has saved
10 marbles from last year. On the first night of the year,
she receives 2 marbles. Leeyan continues to receive
2 marbles each night for the first 30 nights of the year.

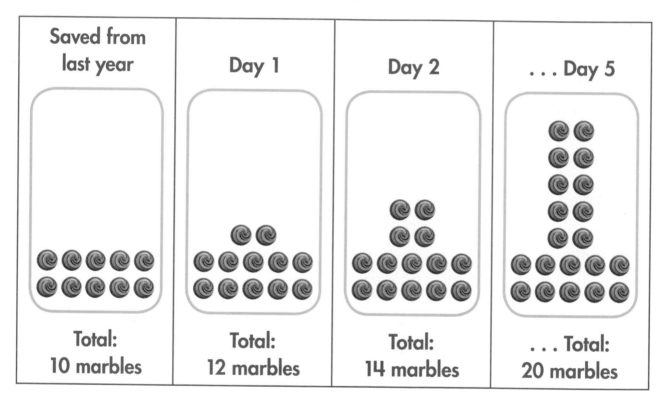

Saved from last year	Day 1	Day 2	. . . Day 5
Total: 10 marbles	Total: 12 marbles	Total: 14 marbles	. . . Total: 20 marbles

The Magic Marbles of Rhomaar (page 3 of 6)

How Many Marbles?

Leeyan had 10 Magic Marbles left from the year before.
She was given 2 Magic Marbles each night for 30 nights.
How many marbles does Leeyan have on the tenth day?

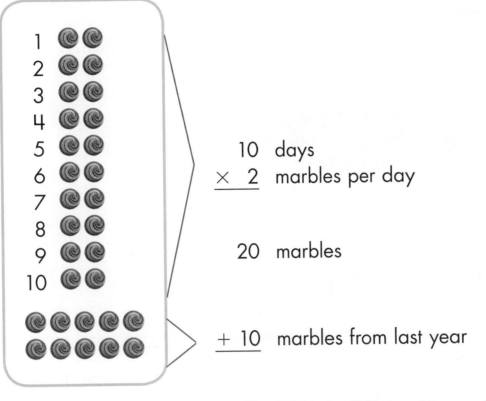

10   days
× 2   marbles per day

20   marbles

+ 10   marbles from last year

30 **total marbles** on the tenth day

How many marbles does Leeyan have on the twelfth day? How did you figure that out?

The Magic Marbles of Rhomaar (page 4 of 6)

Math Words
- **table**
- **column**
- **row**

Looking at a Table

A table is a way to organize information.

Leeyan had 10 Magic Marbles left from the year before. She was given 2 Magic Marbles each night for 30 nights.

This table shows how many marbles Leeyan has after every 5 days.

Columns go up and down.

Number of Days	Total Number of Marbles
Beginning	10
1	12
2	14
3	16
4	18
5	20
10	30
15	?

Rows go across.

This row shows that, after the fifth day, Leeyan has 20 marbles.

Beginning here, the table skips some rows.

How many marbles does Leeyan have on the fifteenth day? How did you figure that out?

The Magic Marbles of Rhomaar (page 5 of 6)

Looking at a Table, *continued*

Leeyan had 10 Magic Marbles left from the year before. She was given 2 Magic Marbles each night for 30 nights.

This table shows how many marbles Leeyan has after every 5 days.

Number of Days	Total Number of Marbles
Beginning	10
5	20
10	30
15	40
20	50
25	60
30	?

This row shows that, after the twentieth day, Leeyan will have 50 marbles.

How many marbles does Leeyan have on the thirtieth day? How did you figure that out?

The Magic Marbles of Rhomaar (page 6 of 6)

Looking at a Graph

Leeyan had 10 Magic Marbles left from the year before.
She was given 2 Magic Marbles each night for 30 nights.

Here is a graph that shows Leeyan's growing collection of marbles.

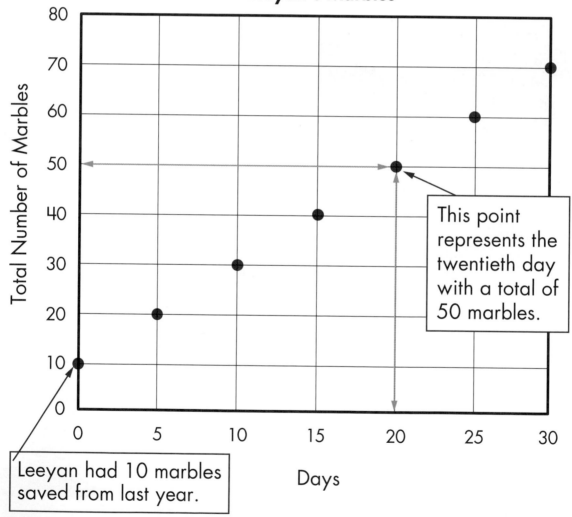

Leeyan's Marbles

This point represents the twentieth day with a total of 50 marbles.

Leeyan had 10 marbles saved from last year.

Why do you think the points on the graph are in a straight line?

Magic Marble Comparisons

(page 1 of 6)

Leeyan had 10 Magic Marbles left from the year before.
She was given 2 Magic Marbles each night for 30 nights.

Sujo had no Magic Marbles left from the year before.
She was given 2 Magic Marbles each night for 30 nights.

Will we ever have the same number of marbles on the
same day?

Day	Leeyan	Sujo
Beginning	10	0
Day 5	20	10
Day 10	30	20
Day 15	40	30
Day 20	50	40
Day 25	60	50
Day 30	70	60

Magic Marble Comparisons

(page 2 of 6)

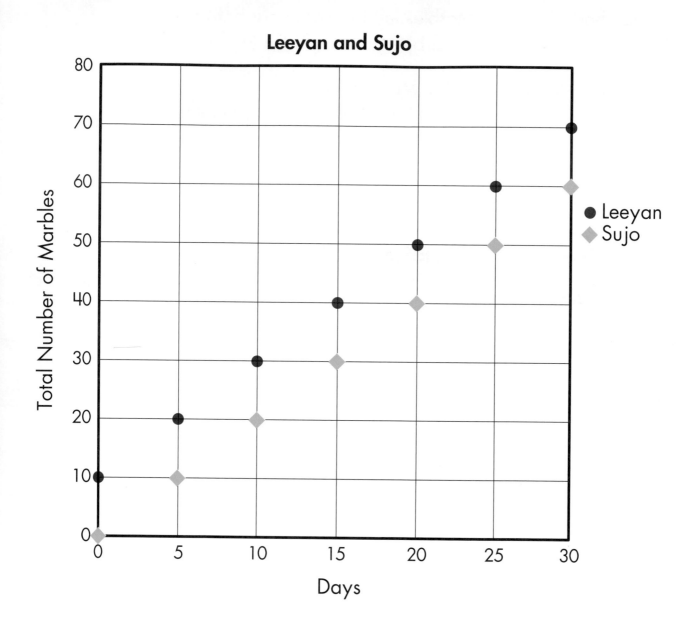

If Leeyan and Sujo keep getting 2 marbles each for 30 more nights, will they ever have the same number of marbles on the same day? How does the table show that? How does the graph show that?

Magic Marble Comparisons

(page 3 of 6)

Leeyan had 10 Magic Marbles left from the year before.
She was given 2 Magic Marbles each night for 30 nights.

Marzig also had 10 Magic Marbles left from the year before.
He was given 3 Magic Marbles each night for 30 nights.

Will Leeyan and Marzig ever have the same number of marbles
on the same day again after the beginning of the year?

Day	Leeyan	Marzig
Beginning	10	10
Day 5	20	25
Day 10	30	40
Day 15	40	55
Day 20	50	70
Day 25	60	85
Day 30	70	100

Magic Marble Comparisons

(page 4 of 6)

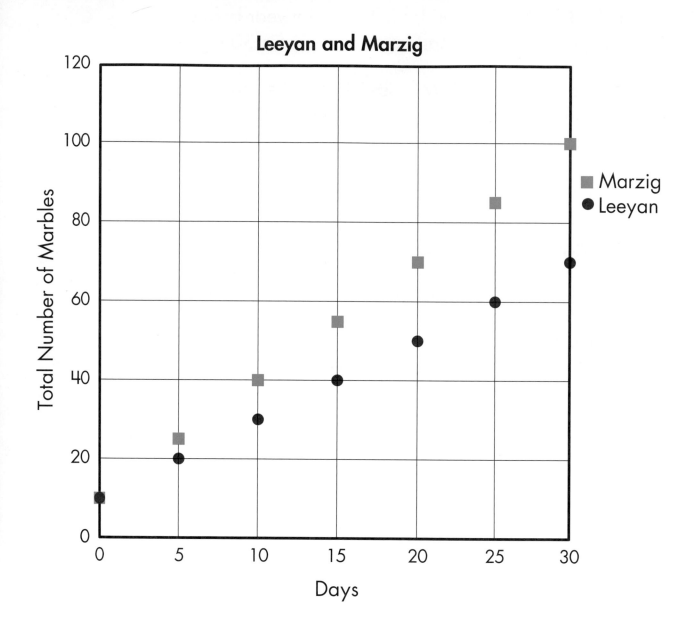

If Leeyan keeps getting 2 marbles each night and Marzig keeps getting 3 marbles each night for 30 more nights, will they ever have the same number of marbles on the same day? How does the table show that? How does the graph show that?

Magic Marble Comparisons

(page 5 of 6)

Leeyan had 10 Magic Marbles left from the year before. She was given 2 Magic Marbles each night for 30 nights.

Bethin had no Magic Marbles left from the year before. She was given 3 Magic Marbles each night for 30 nights.

Do Leeyan and Bethin ever have the same number of marbles on the same day?

Day	Leeyan	Bethin
Beginning	10	0
Day 5	20	15
Day 10	30	30
Day 15	40	45
Day 20	50	60
Day 25	60	75
Day 30	70	90

Magic Marble Comparisons

(page 6 of 6)

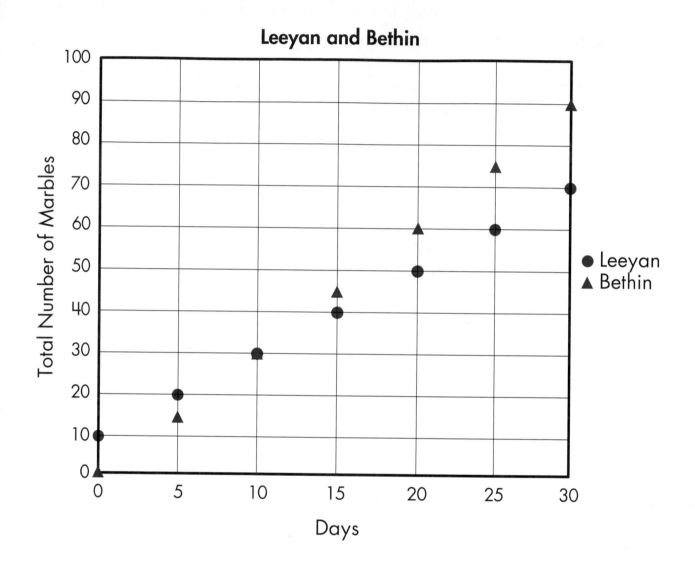

Do Leeyan and Bethin ever have the same number of marbles on the same day? How does the table show that? How does the graph show that? If Leeyan keeps getting 2 marbles each night and Bethin keeps getting 3 marbles each night for 30 more nights, will they ever have the same number of marbles on the same day again? How do you know?

Writing Rules to Describe Change

Tharna had 5 Magic Marbles left from the year before.
She was given 3 Magic Marbles each night for 30 nights.
How many marbles does Tharna have on the tenth day?

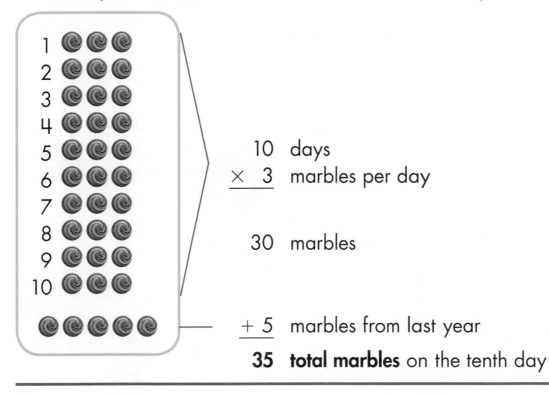

10   days
× 3   marbles per day

30   marbles

+ 5   marbles from last year

35   total marbles on the tenth day

Tharna wrote this rule about her marbles.

I multiply the number of days by 3 marbles per day, and
then add on the 5 marbles that I had left from last year.
That tells me the number of marbles I have on any day.

Number of Days x 3 + 5

Does Tharna's rule work for the total number of marbles on the tenth day? Can you use Tharna's rule to find out how many marbles she will have on the thirtieth day? Make a table or a graph of Tharna's marbles to check.

Working with Data

Math Words
• **data**

Data are pieces of information. You can collect data by counting something, measuring something, or doing experiments.

People collect data to find out about the world around them.

By collecting, representing, and analyzing data, you can answer questions such as these:

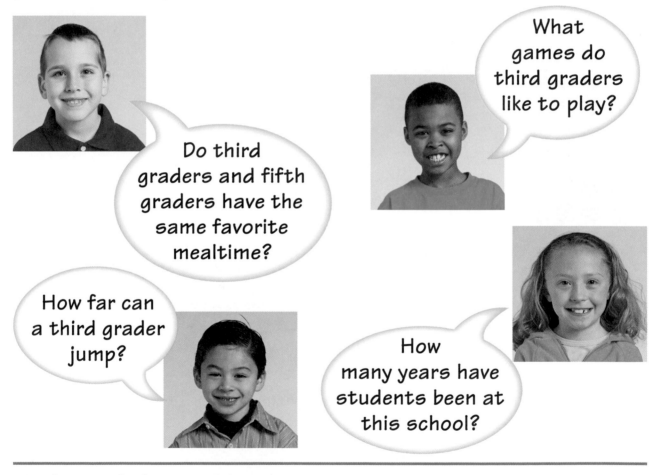

What games do third graders like to play?

Do third graders and fifth graders have the same favorite mealtime?

How far can a third grader jump?

How many years have students been at this school?

Working with data is a process.

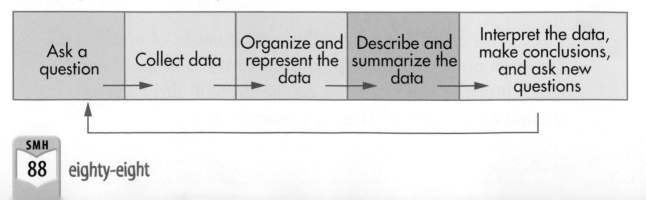

Ask a question	Collect data	Organize and represent the data	Describe and summarize the data	Interpret the data, make conclusions, and ask new questions

Collecting Data

Math Words
• survey

Keisha wondered:

What games do third graders like to play?

She took a survey of her class and collected this set of data.

What is your favorite game?			
Jane	Checkers	Ines	Four Square
Arthur	Jump Rope	Kathryn	Badminton
Beatriz	Table Tennis	Keith	Hide and Seek
Becky	Tag	Kenji	Chinese Checkers
Chiang	Hopscotch	Dwayne	Capture the Flag
Denzel	Go Fish	Keisha	Softball
Deondra	Crazy Eights	Nancy	Kickball
Edwin	Soccer	Nicholas	Red Rover
Elena	Baseball	Philip	Red Light, Green Light
Gil	Mancala	Zhang	Chess

Putting Data Into Categories (page 1 of 2)

Putting data into categories can help you learn something about the group you surveyed.

This was Keisha's first question:

Where do students play their favorite games?

	Tag	
	Hopscotch	
	Capture the Flag	Table Tennis
	Hide and Seek	Crazy Eights
	Four Square	Go Fish
Badminton	Jump Rope	Checkers
Baseball	Kickball	Mancala
Soccer	Red Light, Green Light	Chess
Softball	Red Rover	Chinese Checkers
Sports: Fields and Courts	**Playground Games**	**Games You Can Play Inside**

Keisha noticed:

Almost half of the class like games played on the playground.

Putting Data Into Categories (page 2 of 2)

This was Keisha's second question:

Do students play their favorite games alone, with a partner, or with a group?

		Tag
		Baseball
	Mancala	Softball
	Table Tennis	Soccer
	Badminton	Four Square
	Chinese Checkers	Hide and Seek
	Crazy Eights	Red Rover
	Go Fish	Red Light, Green Light
Hopscotch	Checkers	Capture the Flag
Jump Rope	Chess	Kickball
Games You Can Play Alone	**Games You Play with a Partner**	**Games You Play with a Group**

Keisha noticed:

Almost all the students like games that they play with other people.

What other categories can you make using these data?

Reading and Interpreting a Bar Graph

Keisha wondered where all of the third graders at her school like to play their favorite games. She collected data from the other Grade 3 classes.

Her data are shown in this bar graph.

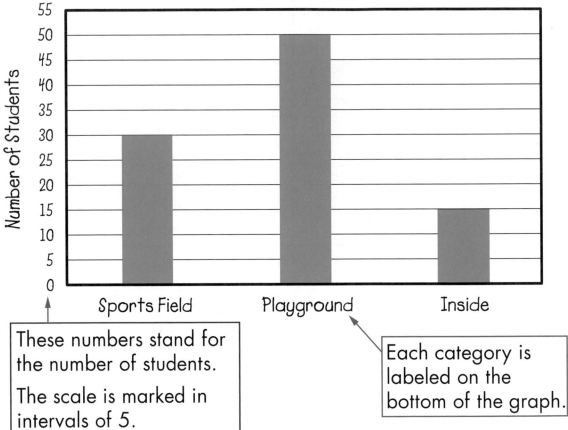

Places We Like To Play

These numbers stand for the number of students.

The scale is marked in intervals of 5.

Each category is labeled on the bottom of the graph.

The middle bar shows that 50 third graders prefer to play at the playground.

More Than Half, Less Than Half

These phrases are useful to describe and summarize data:

Almost all the data...

Very few of the data...

About half the data...

More than half the data...

Less than half the data...

Keisha shared her data with her class.

The teacher asked, "What can you say about the places that third graders like to play?"

Here are some of the students' responses.

Very few of the students prefer to play inside.

About half of the students prefer to play at a playground.

Less than half of the students prefer to play at a sports field.

Almost all of the students like to play outside, either at a sports field or at a playground.

How would you describe the places where these third graders like to play?

Reading and Interpreting a Double-Bar Graph

Math Words
- **double-bar graph**
- **key**

Keisha wanted to compare the places third graders like to play with the places first graders like to play. She collected data from the Grade 1 classes at her school.

Her data are shown on this double-bar graph.

The key shows that the blue bars are third graders' responses and the purple bars are first graders' responses.

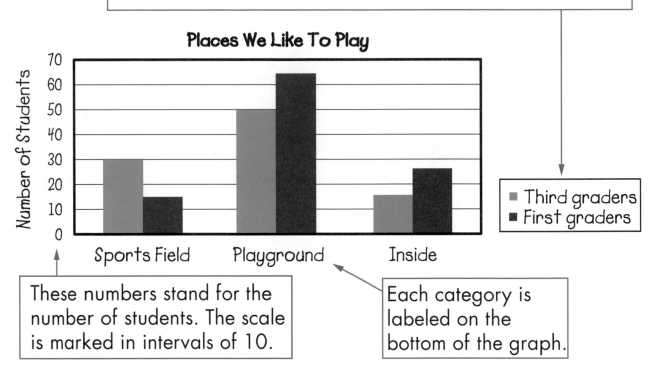

Places We Like To Play

Number of Students

Third graders
First graders

Sports Field   Playground   Inside

These numbers stand for the number of students. The scale is marked in intervals of 10.

Each category is labeled on the bottom of the graph.

The middle bars show that 50 third graders prefer to play at a playground and 65 first graders prefer to play at a playground.

? Compare the places third graders like to play and the places first graders like to play. How are they the same or different? What may be some reasons for the similarities or differences?

Organizing and Representing Data (page 1 of 2)

Becky wondered:

How many states have third graders visited?

She took a survey of her class and collected this set of data:

How many states have you visited?			
Jane 3	Deondra 2	Kathryn 7	Nancy 3
Arthur 4	Edwin 1	Keith 8	Nicholas 3
Beatriz 1	Elena 3	Kenji 2	Philip 1
Becky 2	Gil 14	Dwayne 2	Zhang 5
Chiang 3	Ines 1	Murphy 8	
Denzel 8	Jung 4	Keisha 7	

Becky decided to organize and represent the data in several different ways.

First she organized the data by using tally marks.

Number of states	Number of students
1	IIII
2	IIII
3	IIIII
4	II
5	I
7	II
8	III
14	I

Organizing and Representing Data (page 2 of 2)

Then Becky represented the data in a line plot.

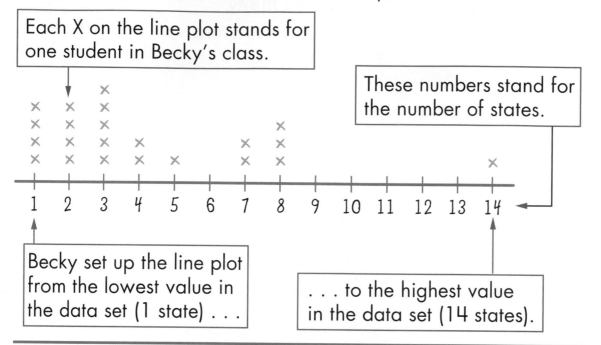

Each X on the line plot stands for one student in Becky's class.

These numbers stand for the number of states.

Becky set up the line plot from the lowest value in the data set (1 state) . . .

. . . to the highest value in the data set (14 states).

She also represented the data in a bar graph.

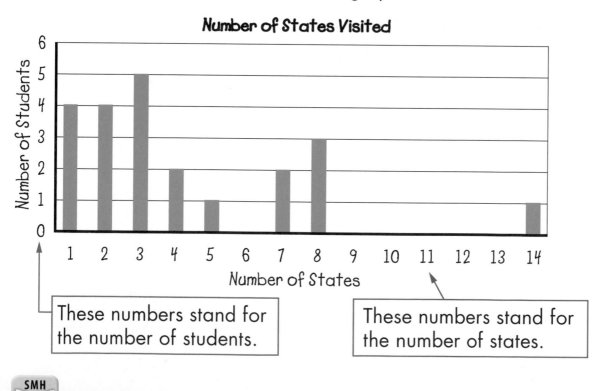

Number of States Visited

These numbers stand for the number of students.

These numbers stand for the number of states.

Describing and Summarizing Data (page 1 of 2)

Math Words
• mode

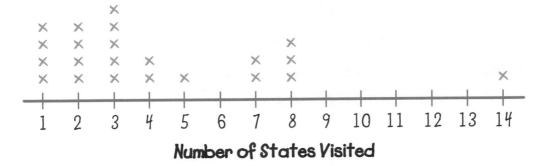

Number of States Visited

Becky shared her data with her class.

The teacher asked, *"What can you say about the number of states visited by students in our class?"*

Here are some of the students' responses:

Gina noticed the lowest and highest values in this data set.

> **Gina:** *The data range from 1 state to 14 states. No one in our class visited fewer than 1 state and no one visited more than 14 states.*

Kenji found an interval where most of the data are concentrated.

> **Kenji:** *More than half of the class visited between 1 state and 3 states.*

Pilar noticed the mode in this data set.

> **Pilar:** *More people visited 3 states than any other number of states.*

> The mode is the value that occurs most often in a set of data.

Describing and Summarizing Data (page 2 of 2)

Oscar noticed an outlier in this data set.

Oscar: *One person visited 14 states and 14 states is far away from the rest of the data. Visiting 14 states is unusual for our class, since most people visited between 1 and 3 states.*

An outlier is a piece of data that has an unusual value, much lower or much higher than most of the data.

Tom noticed a small clump of data.

A few students in our class visited 7 or 8 states. That's more states than most kids visited.

Think about the outlier in Becky's data.
What reasons might there be for one student visiting 14 states?
What do you think the data show about this class?
If you were writing a newspaper article, what would you report?
What evidence from the data supports your ideas?

Comparing Two Sets of Data

(page 1 of 5)

Some of Becky's classmates asked this question:

How do the number of states visited by third graders compare with the number of states visited by fifth graders?

They collected data from a Grade 5 class.

How many states have you visited?

3	7	4	1	6	11
1	3	10	4	9	4
7	5	2	5	1	6
4	5	2	10	7	

They organized the data from the Grade 5 class by using tally marks.

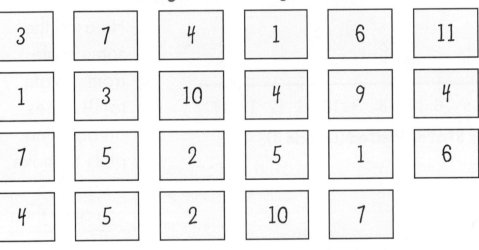

Grade 5	
Number of States	Number of Students
1	III
2	II
3	II
4	IIII
5	III
6	II
7	III
9	I
10	II
11	I

Comparing Two Sets of Data (page 2 of 5)

The students created representations that allowed them to easily compare the data from the Grade 5 class with the data that Becky collected from their Grade 3 class.

Philip represented each set of data on a line plot.

Philip's representation

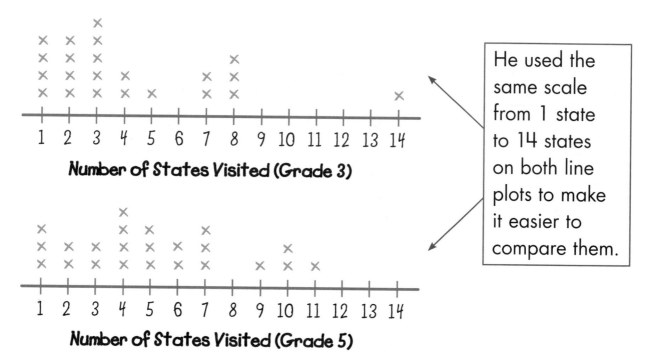

He used the same scale from 1 state to 14 states on both line plots to make it easier to compare them.

Philip: *About half of the fifth graders have visited 5 or more states. Very few of the third graders have visited 5 or more states.*

Comparing Two Sets of Data (page 3 of 5)

Elena represented the data on a double-bar graph.

Elena's representation

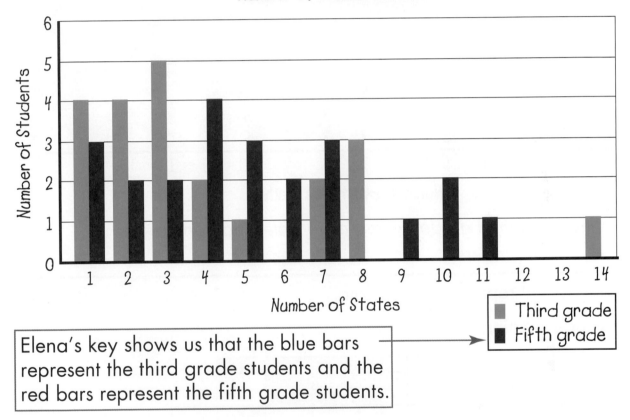

Elena's key shows us that the blue bars represent the third grade students and the red bars represent the fifth grade students.

Elena: *More third graders visited 3 states than any other number of states. More fifth graders visited 4 states than any other number of states.*

Comparing Two Sets of Data (page 4 of 5)

This is how Kelley represented the data. She used the numbers 3 and 5 instead of **X**s to show the different grades.

Kelley's representation

5		5											
5	5	5	5										
5	5	3	5			5							
3	3	3	5	5		5							
3	3	3	5	5		5	3						
3	3	3	3	5	5	3	3		5				
3	3	3	3	3	5	3	3	5	5	5			3
1	2	3	4	5	6	7	8	9	10	11	12	13	14

Number of States Visited

Kelley: *One third grader visited more states than any of the fifth graders.*

This is how Gil represented the data.

Gil's representation

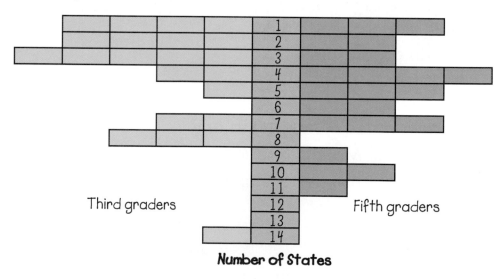

Number of States

Gil: *Four fifth graders visited 9 or more states. Only one third grader visited more than 9 states.*

Comparing Two Sets of Data (page 5 of 5)

Math Words
• median

Keith found the median for each set of data.

The median is the middle value of the data when all the data are put in order.

Keith's representation: Here are all the data from **Grade 5** listed in order:

1, 1, 1, 2, 2, 3, 3, 4, 4, 4, 4, 5, 5, 5, 6, 6, 7, 7, 7, 9, 10, 10, 11

↑
median
The middle value is 5.
The median value is 5 states.

Half of the fifth graders visited 5 states or less and half of them visited 5 states or more.

Here are all the data from **Grade 3** listed in order:

1, 1, 1, 1, 2, 2, 2, 2, 3, 3, 3, 3, 3, 4, 4, 5, 7, 7, 8, 8, 8, 14

↑
median
The middle two values are 3.
The median value is 3 states.

Half of the third graders visited 3 states or less and half of them visited 3 states or more.

Keith: *The median for the Grade 3 data (3 states) is lower than the median for the Grade 5 data (5 states). Overall, fifth graders traveled to more states than third graders.*

Compare the number of states visited by third graders and fifth graders. How are they the same or different? What may be some reasons for the similarities or differences?

Linear Measurement

By measuring length, you can answer questions such as these.

How tall am I?

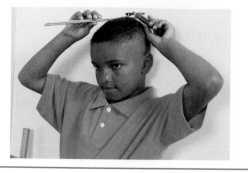

How wide is this bookshelf?

What is the perimeter of the soccer field?

There are two different systems of measuring length.

People in the United States use the U.S. standard system to measure most lengths using inches, feet, yards, and miles. Two other countries, Liberia and Myanmar, use this measurement system.	People from most other countries around the world use the metric system for measuring lengths using millimeters, centimeters, meters, and kilometers.

- During Unit 2, *Surveys and Line Plots*, you will collect data by measuring length in inches, feet, and yards.
- During Unit 4, *Perimeter, Angles, and Area*, you will learn more about both the U.S. standard system and the metric system.

Measurement Benchmarks in the U.S. Standard System

Math Words
- inch
- foot
- yard

Things that are *about* the same length as . . .

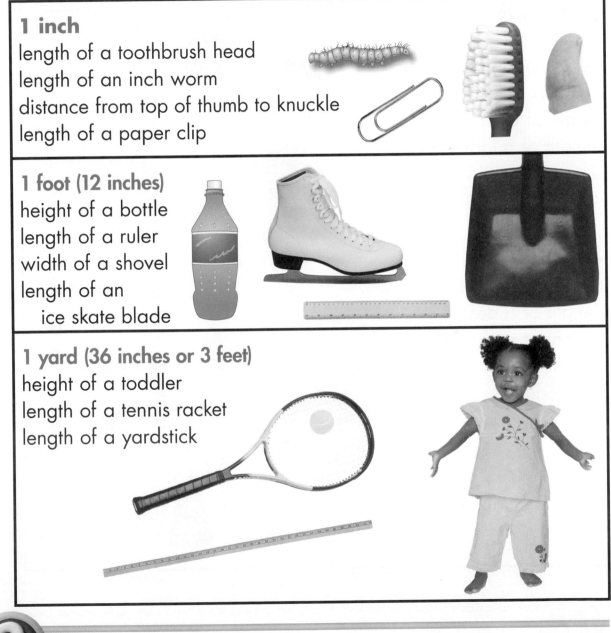

1 inch
length of a toothbrush head
length of an inch worm
distance from top of thumb to knuckle
length of a paper clip

1 foot (12 inches)
height of a bottle
length of a ruler
width of a shovel
length of an
   ice skate blade

1 yard (36 inches or 3 feet)
height of a toddler
length of a tennis racket
length of a yardstick

Can you find some other things that are about the length of an inch, a foot, or a yard?

Measurement Benchmarks in the Metric System

Things that are *about* the same length as . . .

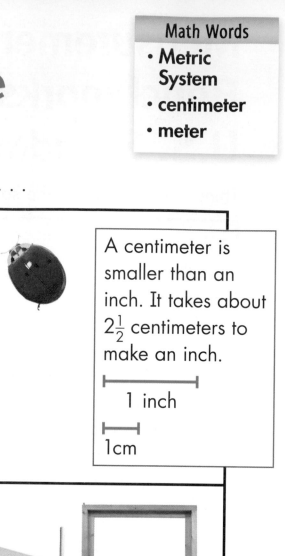

1 centimeter
width of a fingernail
length of an uncooked
   black bean
width of a top of pencil eraser
length of a lady bug

A centimeter is smaller than an inch. It takes about $2\frac{1}{2}$ centimeters to make an inch.

| 1 inch |

1cm

1 meter (100 centimeters)
length of a desk
height of a window
length of a broom
   handle
length of a meterstick

A meter is a little longer than a yard.

? Find something that is about the length of a centimeter or meter. What did you find?

Measurement Tools

A ruler is a tool to measure length.

This ruler measures inches on one side and centimeters on the other side.

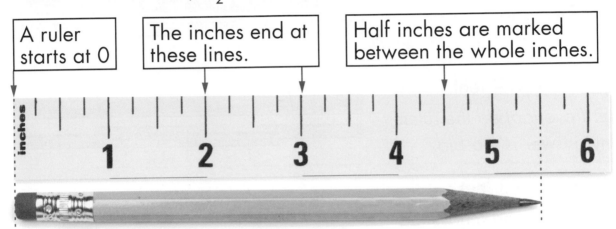

This ruler is 6 inches (or $\frac{1}{2}$ foot) long. It is about 15 centimeters long.

| A ruler starts at 0 | The inches end at these lines. | Half inches are marked between the whole inches. |

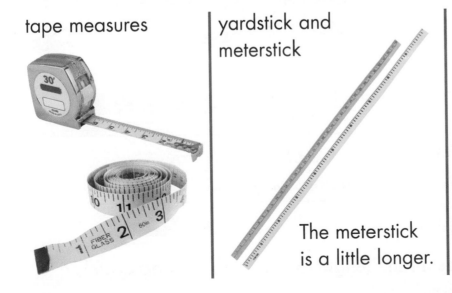

The pencil starts at 0 and ends between 5 and 6. It is $5\frac{1}{2}$ inches long.

Here are some other measuring tools.

tape measures

yardstick and meterstick

odometer

The meterstick is a little longer.

An odometer measures the distance a car has traveled in miles or kilometers.

Measuring Accurately

The students in Ms. Smith's class used rulers to measure the length of the chalk tray in their classroom. Even though the students measured the same distance, they got several different answers.

Look at the pictures below and look for the measurement mistakes the students made.

Becky measured 3 feet.

Becky: *I left gaps between the rulers, so my answer is too small.*

Kenji measured 4 feet.

Kenji: *I overlapped the rulers, so my answer is too big.*

Pilar measured 3 feet.

Pilar: *I didn't start measuring at the beginning of the chalk tray and I didn't measure all the way to the end.*

Oscar measured 4 feet.

Oscar: *I didn't keep the rulers straight.*

Nancy measured $3\frac{1}{2}$ feet.

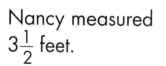
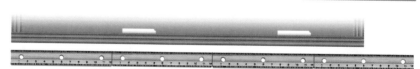

Nancy: *I lined up the ruler to the left side of the chalk tray. My rulers lined up exactly with no overlaps or gaps.*

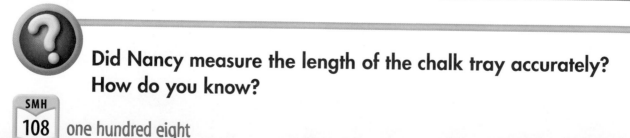

Did Nancy measure the length of the chalk tray accurately? How do you know?

Measuring With Inches and Feet

During Unit 2, *Surveys and Line Plots,* you will collect data to answer this question:

How far can a third grader jump?

These four students jumped with both feet. They measured their jumps by putting rulers end to end.

Nancy's jump measured 4 rulers.

She jumped 4 feet or 12 + 12 + 12 + 12 = **48 inches.**

Chiang's jump measured 3 rulers and 2 more inches.

She jumped 3 feet 2 inches or 12 + 12 + 12 + 2 = **38 inches.**

Denzel's jump measured 1 yardstick and 11 inches.

He jumped 3 feet 11 inches or 36 + 11 = **47 inches.**

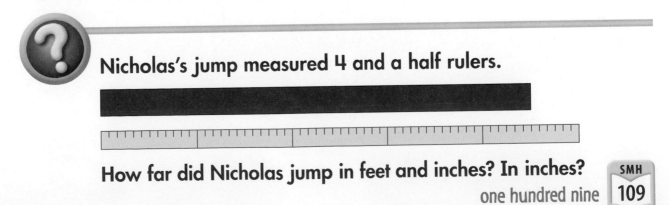

Nicholas's jump measured 4 and a half rulers.

How far did Nicholas jump in feet and inches? In inches?

Perimeter (page 1 of 2)

Math Words
• perimeter

Perimeter is the length of the border of a figure.
Perimeter is a linear measure.

An ant walks around the perimeter of this photograph by starting at one corner, walking all the way around the border, and ending at the same corner where it started.

How far did the ant walk?

What is the perimeter of this photograph?

Perimeter (page 2 of 2)

Kenji:

I measured the sides of the photograph using inches.

$2 + 3 + 2 + 3 = 10$

The perimeter of the photograph is **10 inches.**

2 inches

3 inches

3 inches

2 inches

about 5 centimeters

about $7\frac{1}{2}$ centimeters

Nancy:

I measured the sides of the photograph using centimeters.

The top measured about 5 centimeters.

The bottom will measure the same as the top.

The left side measured about $7\frac{1}{2}$ centimeters.

The right side will measure the same as the left side.

$7\frac{1}{2} + 5 = 12\frac{1}{2}$

$12\frac{1}{2} + 12\frac{1}{2} = 25$

The perimeter of the photograph is about **25 centimeters.**

Why is the answer in inches different than the answer in centimeters?

Solving Perimeter Problems (page 1 of 2)

Fill in the missing measures and find the perimeter.

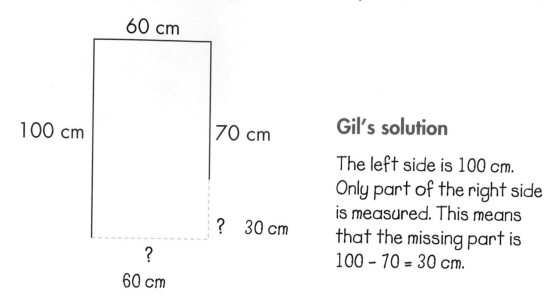

Gil's solution

The left side is 100 cm. Only part of the right side is measured. This means that the missing part is 100 – 70 = 30 cm.

The bottom measure is just like the top measure.

The perimeter is 100 + 60 + 70 + 30 + 60 = **320 cm.**

Figure out the dimensions for a rectangle with a perimeter of 200 meters.

Deondra's solution

If the perimeter is 200 meters, then half way around is 100 meters. The top and side measures of the rectangle must equal 100 meters; for example 80 + 20.

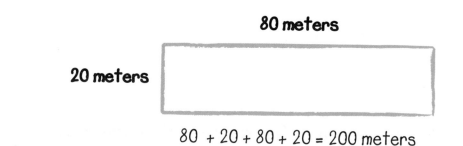

80 + 20 + 80 + 20 = 200 meters

Solving Perimeter Problems (page 2 of 2)

> Use the *LogoPaths* software to solve problems about perimeter.

What is the perimeter of the reading table?

Ines's Solution

Since the reading table is curved, I wrapped a piece of string around the border of the table and then I measured the length of the string.

The perimeter of the reading table is **5 yards**.

Area

Area is the measure of a surface—for example, the amount of flat space a figure covers. Area is a measure of 2-D space. Area is often measured in square units, like square centimeters or square feet.

Gina and her mother plan to make a patchwork quilt. Here is a sketch of their quilt design.

5 feet

3 feet

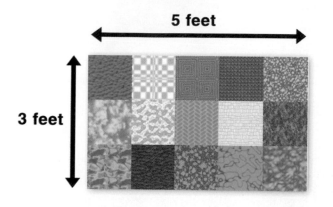

The quilt is made up of squares.

What is the area of the quilt?
How many squares do they need?

Jung's solution

*The area of the quilt is 15 square feet.
They need* **15 squares.**

The area of this 12 by 10 rectangle is 120 square units.

10

12

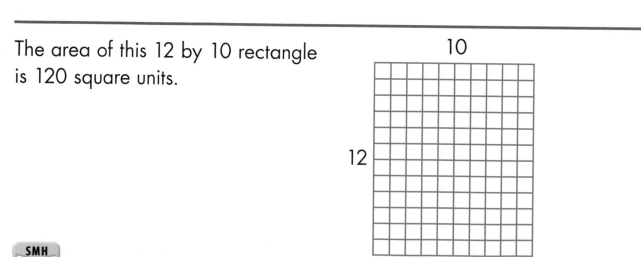

Measuring Area Using Square Units

Philip drew some figures on dot paper.

He counted the square units inside each figure using squares and triangles.

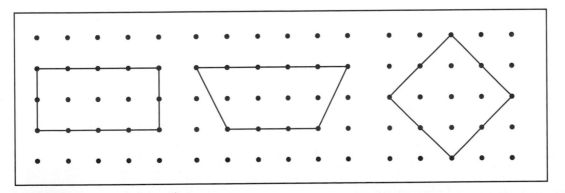

| 1 square unit is shaded. | $\frac{1}{2}$ square unit is shaded. | 1 square unit is shaded. |

1 square unit is split into 2 triangles that are the same size; each triangle is $\frac{1}{2}$ square unit.

2 square units are split into 2 triangles that are the same size; each triangle is 1 square unit.

Philip: *The area of all of these figures is the same. They each measure 8 square units.*

Do you agree with Philip's statements?
Does each of these figures measure 8 square units?

Dominoes, Triominoes, and Tetrominoes

Here are some figures made up of square units.

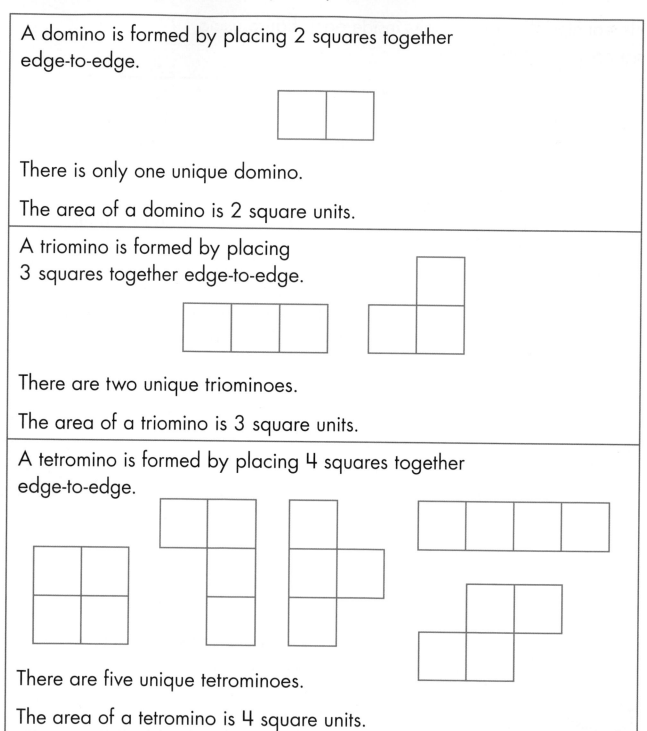

A domino is formed by placing 2 squares together edge-to-edge.

There is only one unique domino.

The area of a domino is 2 square units.

A triomino is formed by placing 3 squares together edge-to-edge.

There are two unique triominoes.

The area of a triomino is 3 square units.

A tetromino is formed by placing 4 squares together edge-to-edge.

There are five unique tetrominoes.

The area of a tetromino is 4 square units.

Slide, Turn, and Flip

Look at how this figure moves, using slides, flips, and turns.

Slide:

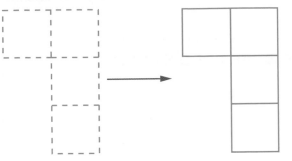

Turn:

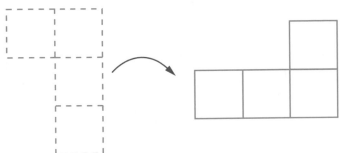

Flip:

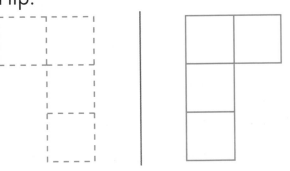

The six figures on this page are all congruent. They have exactly the same size and shape.

When you can move a figure with a slide, a turn, or a flip and it fits exactly on top of another figure, then the figures are congruent.

Read more about congruent figures on page 124.

Polygons

Polygons are closed 2-D figures with straight sides.

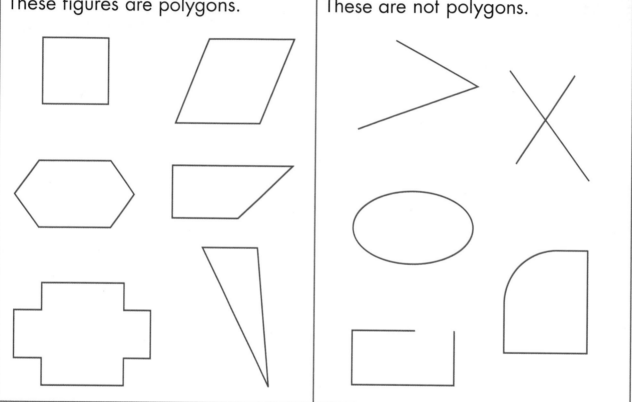

These figures are polygons.

These are not polygons.

Which of these figures are polygons?

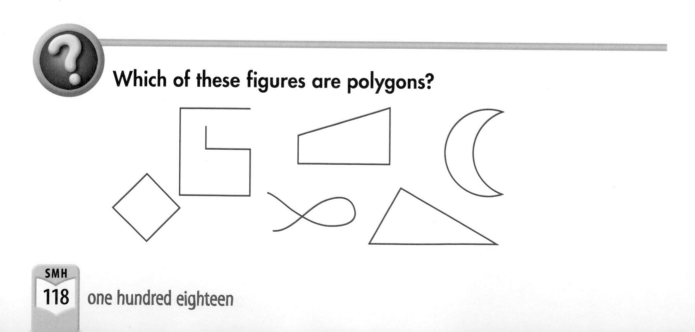

Naming Polygons

Polygons are named for the number of sides they have.

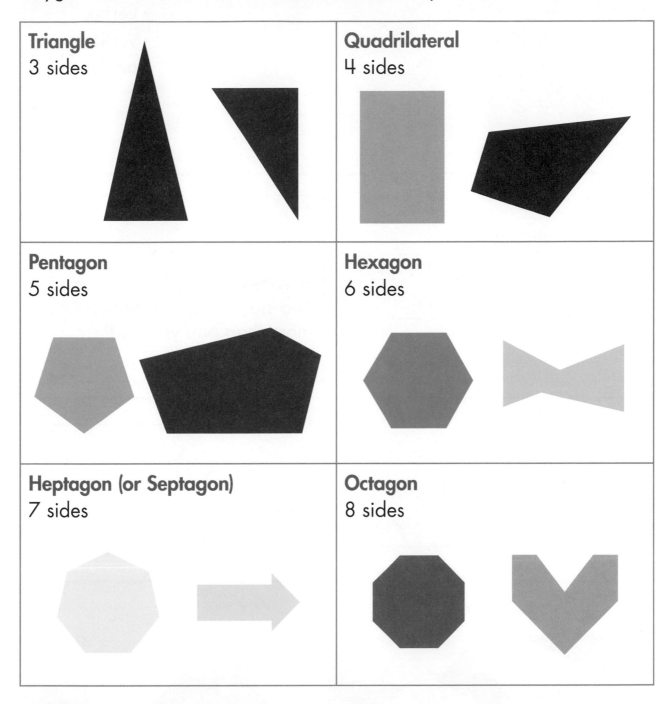

Triangle
3 sides

Quadrilateral
4 sides

Pentagon
5 sides

Hexagon
6 sides

Heptagon (or Septagon)
7 sides

Octagon
8 sides

? A polygon with 12 sides is called a dodecagon.
Can you draw a dodecagon?

Triangles

A triangle is a polygon that . . .

. . . has 3 sides.

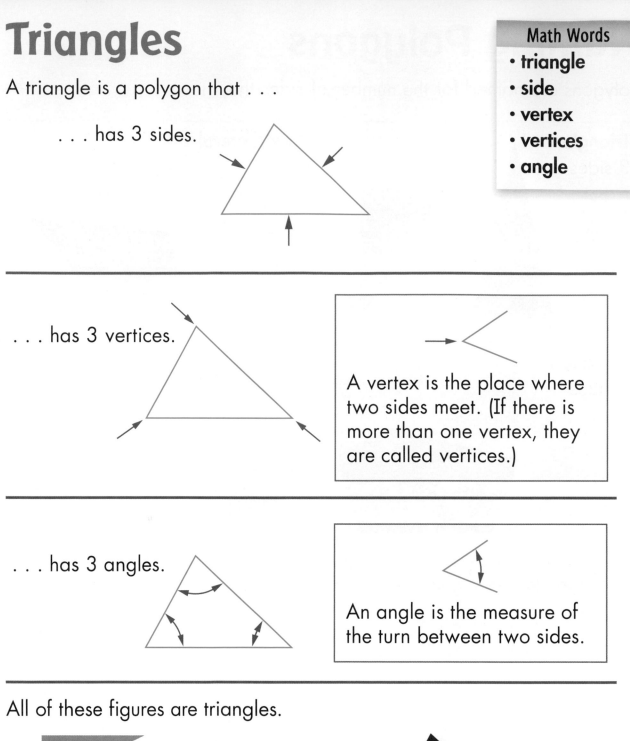

Math Words
- **triangle**
- **side**
- **vertex**
- **vertices**
- **angle**

. . . has 3 vertices.

A vertex is the place where two sides meet. (If there is more than one vertex, they are called vertices.)

. . . has 3 angles.

An angle is the measure of the turn between two sides.

All of these figures are triangles.

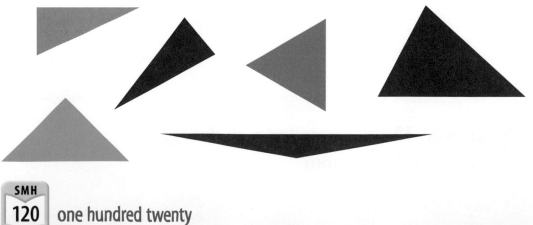

Quadrilaterals

A quadrilateral is a polygon that:

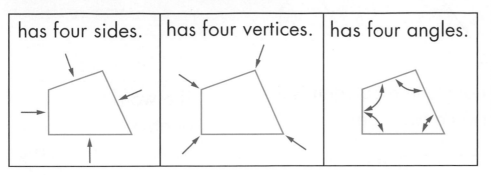

has four sides.	has four vertices.	has four angles.

Math Words
• **quadrilateral**
• **parallelogram**
• **rectangle**
• **rhombus**
• **square**
• **trapezoid**

All of these figures are quadrilaterals. Some quadrilaterals have other special names, too.

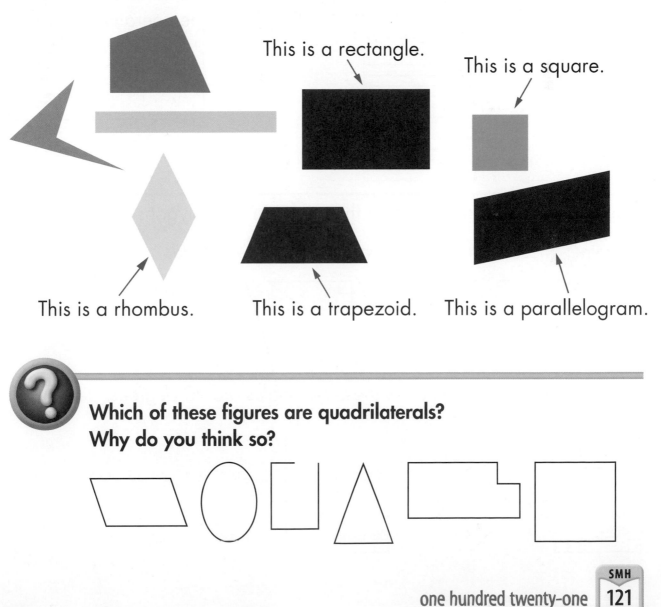

This is a rectangle.

This is a square.

This is a rhombus.

This is a trapezoid.

This is a parallelogram.

Which of these figures are quadrilaterals? Why do you think so?

Angles (page 1 of 2)

Math Words
- **degree**
- **right angle**

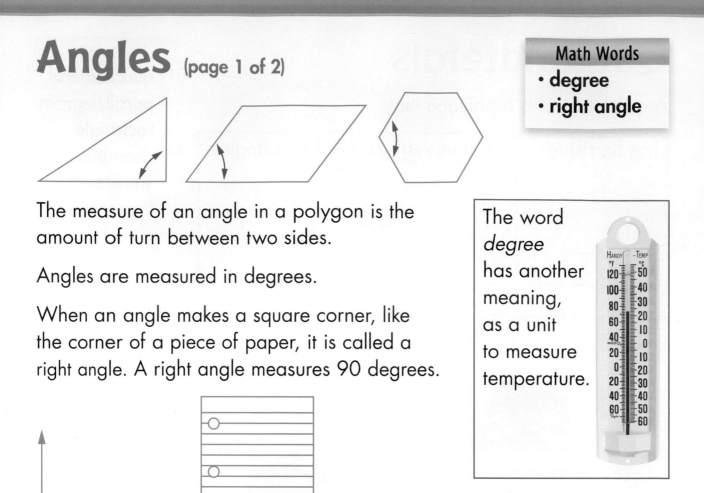

The measure of an angle in a polygon is the amount of turn between two sides.

Angles are measured in degrees.

When an angle makes a square corner, like the corner of a piece of paper, it is called a right angle. A right angle measures 90 degrees.

The word *degree* has another meaning, as a unit to measure temperature.

These students are talking about the angles in the polygons they drew.

Dwayne: *These triangles all have one 90-degree angle.*

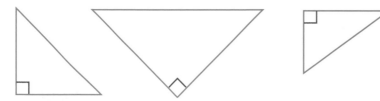

Jung: *All of the angles in all of these rectangles are 90 degrees.*

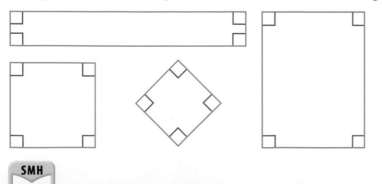

Angles (page 2 of 2)

Kelley: *I drew this figure that looks like the red trapezoid pattern block. None of the angles are right angles.*

Use the *LogoPaths* software to solve problems about angles.

This angle is greater than 90 degrees.
It is larger than the corner of the paper.

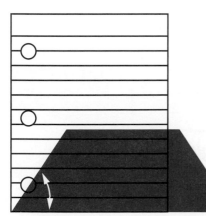

This angle is less than 90 degrees.
It is smaller than the corner of the paper.

Look at these figures. Where do you see right angles?
Where do you see angles that are smaller than a right angle?
Where do you see angles that are larger than a right angle?

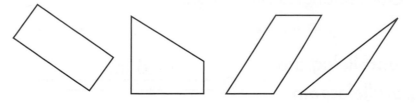

Congruent Figures

Math Words
• **congruent**

Two figures are congruent if they are exactly the same size and shape.

These students are comparing the figures they built with straws.

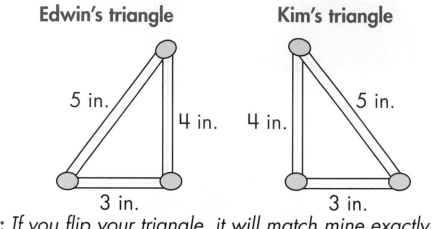

Edwin's triangle   **Kim's triangle**

5 in.   4 in.   4 in.   5 in.

3 in.   3 in.

Kim: *If you flip your triangle, it will match mine exactly.
Our triangles are congruent.*

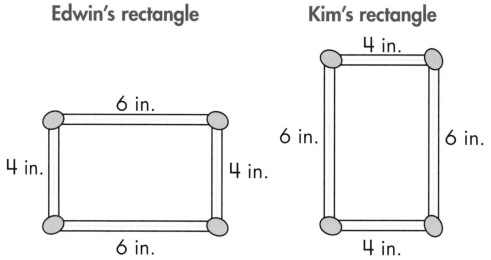

Edwin's rectangle   **Kim's rectangle**

4 in.

6 in.   6 in.   6 in.

4 in.   4 in.

6 in.   4 in.

Edwin: *Your rectangle looks like my rectangle turned
on its side. Our rectangles are congruent.*

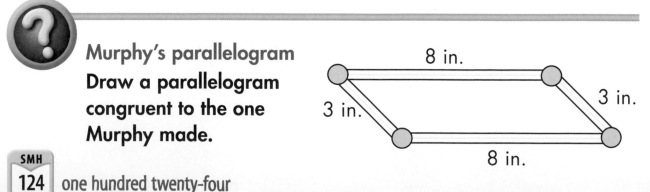

Murphy's parallelogram
**Draw a parallelogram
congruent to the one
Murphy made.**

8 in.

3 in.   3 in.

8 in.

Geometric Solids (page 1 of 2)

Math Words
• **three-dimensional (3-D)**

A geometric solid is a figure that has three dimensions—length, width, and height. We say that it is three-dimensional (3-D).

Here are pictures and sketches of the set of geometric solids you are using at school.

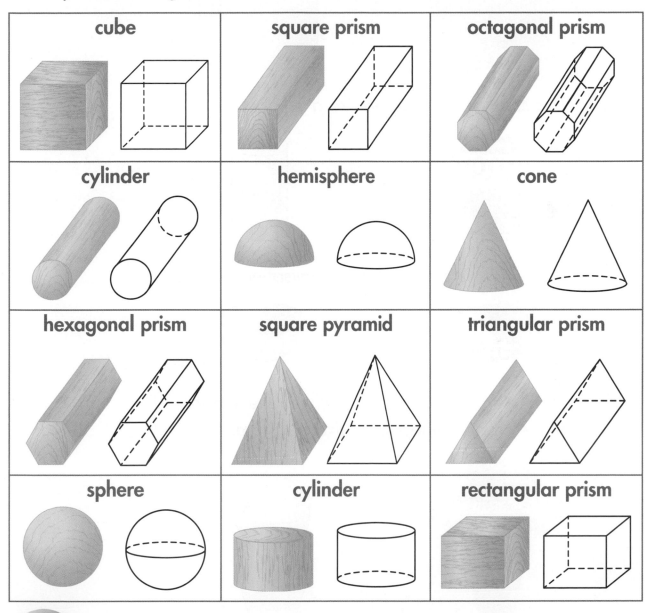

cube	square prism	octagonal prism
cylinder	hemisphere	cone
hexagonal prism	square pyramid	triangular prism
sphere	cylinder	rectangular prism

What real-world objects are shaped like these geometric solids?

Geometric Solids (page 2 of 2)

Pilar noticed these objects in her kitchen that looked like the solids her class had been studying in school.

Pilar: *This toaster is shaped like a rectangular prism.*

 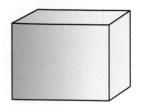

This soup can is shaped like a cylinder.

 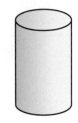

Dad's wok is shaped like a hemisphere.

My ice cream cone is a cone and the scoop of ice cream on top looks like a sphere.

Describing Geometric Solids (page 1 of 2)

Math Words
- **edge**
- **face**
- **vertex**

One way to describe a geometric solid is to identify the number of faces, edges, and vertices it has.

How many faces does this number cube have?

A face is the 2-D figure that makes up a side of a 3-D solid.

When you roll a number cube, it can come up on six different numbers, so it has six faces.

1 2 3
4 5 6

Oscar built a cube, using straws and clay.

How many edges does it have?

Each straw is one edge of the cube. There are 4 straws on top, 4 on the bottom, and 4 that go up and down. There are 12 edges.

An edge is the line segment where two faces meet.

How many vertices does it have?

Each piece of clay is at one vertex. There are 4 pieces of clay on top and 4 on the bottom. There are 8 vertices.

A vertex is the point at the corner where edges meet.

Describing Geometric Solids (page 2 of 2)

The square pyramid has 5 faces. There is 1 square on the bottom, and there are 4 triangles around the sides.

It has 5 vertices. There are 4 around the bottom and 1 point on top.

It has 8 edges. It took 4 straws to make the square on the bottom. And there are 4 more straws connecting to the top.

We couldn't build the cylinder with straws and clay because the edges are round, not straight, and it doesn't have any corners.

The cylinder has 3 surfaces. There is a circle on the top and a circle on the bottom. The middle part is curved—if you open it up it is a rectangle, like the label on a soup can.

Imagine building this prism with straws and clay. How many faces does it have? What do the faces look like? How many edges does it have? How many vertices does it have?

Sorting Geometric Solids

(page 1 of 2)

Kenji and Bridget are sorting their set of geometric solids into groups. They have found two categories.

Solids With Some Curved Surfaces

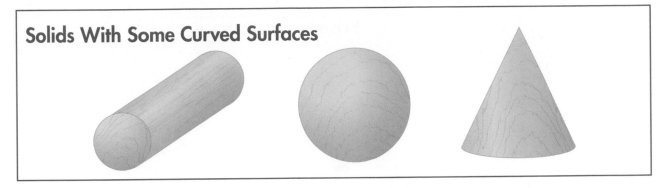

Kenji: *Each of these solids can roll on the table.*

Bridget: *The cone has a flat circle on the bottom, but the rest of it is curved.*

Solids With All Flat Faces

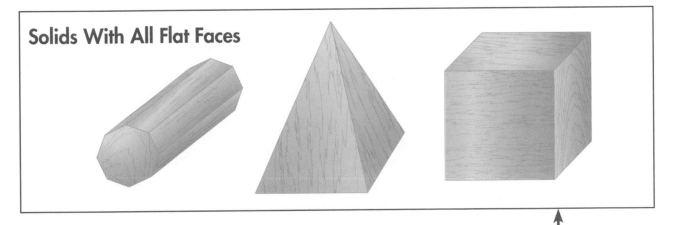

Kenji: *Each face is a polygon.*

Bridget: *None of these faces are curved.*

A polyhedron is a geometric solid that has all flat faces.

Sorting Geometric Solids

(page 2 of 2)

Keith and Kelley found a different way to sort the geometric solids that they built with straws and clay.

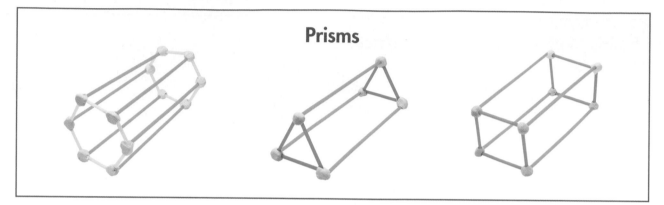

Prisms

Keith: *The top and bottom of each prism match: hexagon and hexagon, triangle and triangle, square and square.*

Kelley: *The faces on the sides of these prisms are all rectangles.*

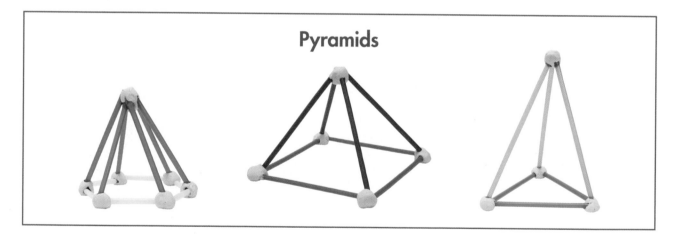

Pyramids

Keith: *The base of each pyramid is a polygon. There is a point at the top of each pyramid.*

Kelley: *The faces on the sides of the pyramids are all triangles.*

? **Some prisms have parallelograms that are not rectangles on the sides. Can you imagine what one of these might look like?**

Nets

Math Words
- **net**

A net is a 2-D pattern that can be folded to make a 3-D figure.

Adam designed a net to cover a square pyramid.

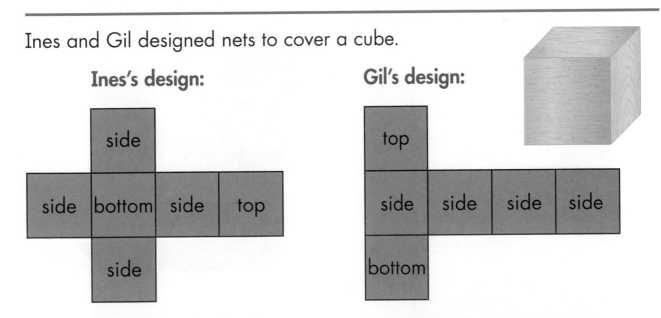

side
side | bottom | side
side

Adam: *My net has 5 polygons because the square pyramid has 5 faces.*

Ines and Gil designed nets to cover a cube.

Ines's design:

side
side | bottom | side | top
side

Gil's design:

top
side | side | side | side
bottom

Ines and Gil: *Since the cube has 6 square faces, each of our nets has 6 squares.*

? Here is a folded pattern for an open box that will hold one cube. Design a pattern with 5 squares that will make this open box.

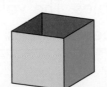

How Many Cubes in a Box? (page 1 of 2)

Math Words
• **volume**

Beatriz and Denzel solved this problem.

Here is a pattern to make an open box. How many cubes will fit exactly in this box?

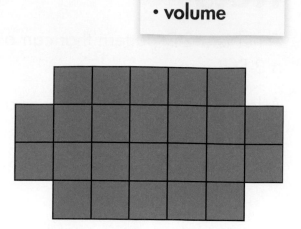

There will be 10 cubes on the bottom layer of the box.

When you fold up the sides, there will be one layer. The box will hold 10 cubes.

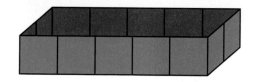

Volume is the amount of space a 3-D object occupies. The volume of a box could be the number of cubes that would completely fill it.

How Many Cubes in a Box? (page 2 of 2)

Nicholas solved this problem.

This is the bottom of an open box that will hold exactly 30 cubes. Draw the sides to complete the pattern for the box.

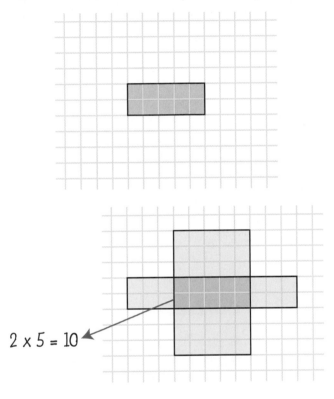

2 x 5 = 10

> Ten cubes will fit on the bottom layer. I drew the sides 3 layers high. The box will look like this.

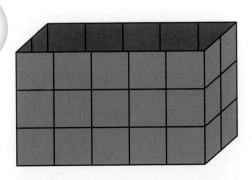

? Design a different box that will also hold 30 cubes.

Games Chart

	Use in Unit	Page
Capture from 300 to 600	8	**G1**
Capture 5	1	**G3**
Capture on the 300 Chart	3	**G4**
Close to 100	1	**G5**
Collect $2.00	1	**G6**
Collections Compare	8	**G7**
Collections Match	3	**G8**
Count and Compare	5	**G9**
Factor Pairs	5	**G10**
Fraction Cookie	7	**G11**
Go Collecting	3	**G13**
How Far from 100?	3	**G15**
Make a Dollar	1	**G16**
Missing Factors	5	**G17**
Practicing with Multiplication Cards	5	**G19**
What's My Shape?	9	**G21**

Capture from 300 to 600

(page 1 of 2)

You need

- 301–600 chart, taped together
- Plus/Minus Cards
- 30 chips
- game piece for each player
- *Capture from 300 to 600* Recording Sheet

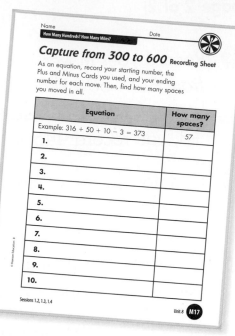

Play in pairs or in 2 teams.

1. Place 30 chips on the 301–600 chart so each chip is on a different number. Deal five Plus/Minus Cards to each player or team and place the remaining cards facedown on the table. Players put their game pieces anywhere on the 301–600 chart to start.

2. Players or teams take turns trying to capture a chip. On your turn, move your game piece using any combination of your Plus/Minus Cards to land on a square with a chip. You can use any number of cards, from one to all five.

3. If you land exactly on a square with a chip, capture it by taking it off the board. You can capture only one chip during a turn, and it must be from the square you land on.

Capture from 300 to 600

(page 2 of 2)

4 Record your moves in an equation on the *Capture from 300–600* Recording Sheet. For example, if you begin on 445 and use the cards +2, +10, −100, and +3, you record 445 + 2 + 10 − 100 + 3 = 360.

5 Find how many spaces you moved altogether, and record that, too. In the example above, you moved forward 15 spaces (+2, +10, and +3) and backward 100 spaces (−100), so altogether you moved backward 85 spaces from 445.

6 Place the Plus/Minus Cards you used facedown in a discard pile. Take cards from the top of the deck to replace them. If the deck of Plus/Minus Cards is used up, shuffle the discard pile and turn it facedown on the table.

7 The first player or team to capture five chips wins.

Capture 5

You need

- 100 chart
- Change Cards (deck of 40)
- 12 chips of one color
- game piece for each player
- *Capture 5* Recording Sheet

Play with a partner, or form a team with your partner and play another team of two players.

1 Place 12 chips on the 100 chart so that each chip is on a different number. Deal five Change Cards to each player or team and place the remaining cards facedown on the table. Players put their game pieces anywhere on the 100 chart to start.

2 Players or teams take turns trying to capture a chip. On your turn, move your game piece by using any combination of your Change Cards to land on a square with a chip. You can use any number of cards, from one to all five.

3 If you land exactly on a square with a chip, capture it by taking it off the board. You can capture only one chip during a turn, and it must be from the square you land on.

4 Record your moves in an equation on the *Capture 5* Recording Sheet. For example, if you begin on 45 and use the cards +2, +10, and +3, you record $45 + 2 + 10 + 3 = 60$.

5 Place the Change Cards you used facedown in a discard pile. Take cards from the top of the deck to replace them. If the deck of Change Cards is used up, shuffle the discard pile and turn it facedown again.

6 The first player or team to capture five chips wins.

Name

Date

Trading Stickers, Combining Coins

Capture 5 Recording Sheet

Record your starting number, the changes you use, and your ending number for each move, like this:

$16 + 10 + 10 - 2 = 34$

M16 Unit 1

Sessions 1.6, 1.7

Capture on the 300 Chart

You need

- 300 chart, taped together
- deck of Plus/Minus Cards
- 30 markers
- game piece for each player
- *Capture on the 300 Chart* Recording Sheet

Play in pairs or in 2 teams.

 Place 30 markers on the 300 chart, each on a different number. Deal 5 to each player or team, and place the remaining cards facedown on the table. Players put game pieces anywhere on the 300 chart.

 On your turn, use any combination of your cards to land on a square with a marker if you can. You can use from one to all five cards.

3 If you land on a square with a marker, capture it by taking it off the board. You can capture only one marker during a turn.

4 Record your moves as an equation.

5 Place the cards you used in a discard pile. Take cards from the deck to replace them. If the deck of cards is used, shuffle the discard pile and start again. The first player or team to capture 5 markers wins.

Close to 100

You need

- Digit Cards (deck of 44)
- *Close to 100* Recording Sheet for each player

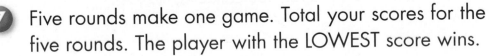

Play alone, with a partner, or in a small group.

1 Deal out six Digit Cards to each player.

2 Use any four cards to make two numbers; for example, 6 and 5 could make either 56 or 65. Wild cards can be used as any numeral. Try to make numbers that, when added, give you a total that is close to 100.

3 Write these two numbers and their total on the *Close to 100* Recording Sheet; for example, 42 + 56 = 98.

4 Find your score. Your score is the difference between your total and 100. For example, if your total is 98, your score is 2. If your total is 105, your score is 5.

5 Put the cards you used in a discard pile. Keep the two cards you did not use for the next round.

6 For the next round, deal four new cards to each player. Make more numbers that come close to 100. When you run out of cards, shuffle the discard pile and use those cards again.

7 Five rounds make one game. Total your scores for the five rounds. The player with the LOWEST score wins.

Collect $2.00

You need

- pennies, dimes, and dollars

- number cube, 1–6 **4**

- number cube, 7–12 **7**

- *Collect $2.00* Recording Sheet

Play with a partner or in a small group.

1 Players take turns rolling the number cubes and collecting the number rolled in coins.

2 After taking the amount rolled, players may trade coins for equivalent amounts if they choose to. For example, a player could trade 10 pennies for 1 dime or 10 dimes for 1 dollar.

3 Players figure out how much money they have after each turn. They record the amount they collected and the total they have on their *Collect $2.00* Recording Sheets.

4 The game is over when each player has collected $2.00.

Collections Compare

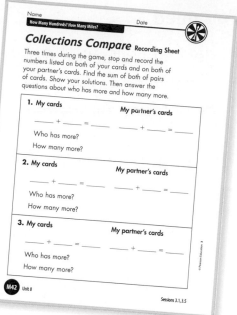

You need

- Collection Cards
  (2 decks; 1 for each player)
- *Collections Compare* Recording Sheet

Play with a partner.

1 Each player shuffles a deck of Collection Cards and places it facedown on the table.

2 To begin the game, each player turns over the first two cards in his or her pile.

3 Determine who has the larger sum. That player takes all four cards. When the larger sum is obvious and both players agree, the player can take the cards without adding. Otherwise, add each pair or use estimation to figure out who has the larger sum.

4 Three times during the game, stop and record. Write the numbers from both players' cards on the *Collections Compare* Recording Sheet. Then answer the questions on the sheet.

5 If players do not agree on the sums of each pair, try a different way of adding each pair of cards.

6 The game ends when the players have turned over all of the cards in the deck. The player with the most cards is the winner.

Collections Match

You need

- deck of Collection Cards
- *Combining Collections: How Many Altogether?*

Play in pairs or in 2 teams.

1 The object is to make matches of Collection Cards from the same category and to find the sum of the two collections in three matches.

2 Lay out 12 Collection Cards facedown on the table, in 3 rows with 4 cards in each row.

3 Take turns turning over two cards from anywhere in the layout. If the two cards are both in the same category, such as dolls, stamps, or trading cards, they are a match and you keep them. If the cards do not match, turn the cards back over and your turn is over.

4 When you collect a match, replace the missing cards with new cards from the deck so that there are always 12 cards to choose from.

5 The player with the most matches when all the cards have been turned over wins the game.

6 When all the cards have been matched, each player chooses three matches to solve for an exact sum. Record the three addition problems on *Combining Collections: How Many Altogether?* and solve each problem.

Count and Compare

You need

- set of Array Cards

Play with a partner or in a small group.

 Deal the Array Cards so that all players have the same number of cards. Set aside any cards that are left over.

 Players place their cards in a stack in front of them with the dimensions side up.

3 Each player places the top card from his or her stack, dimension side up, in the middle of the table.

4 Players decide whose card has the largest array by skip counting, using a known multiplication combination, placing the arrays on top of each other, or some other strategy. Counting the squares by 1s is not allowed.

5 The player with the largest array takes all the cards from the round and places them on the bottom of his or her stack. If all arrays in the round have the same product, players make a rule to determine who gets the cards. When a rule is decided, it cannot be changed until the game is over.

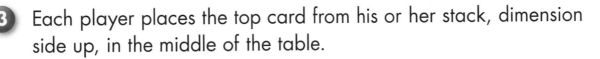

Possible rule: Each player places a second card on top of his or her first one. The player with the largest array of all second cards takes all of the first cards and all of the second cards.

 The game is over when one player runs out of cards. The player with the most cards (or all of the cards) is the winner.

Factor Pairs

You need

- set of Array Cards
- "Combinations I Know" and "Combinations I'm Working On"

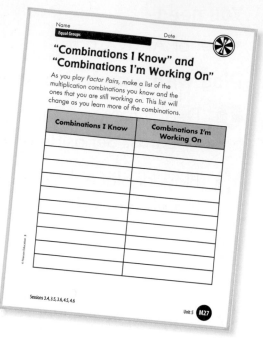

Play alone or with a partner.

1 Spread out all of the Array Cards in front of you with the dimensions side up.

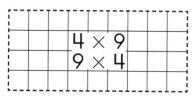

2 Choose an Array Card and put your finger on it. Say the number of squares in the array if you know it. (Do not pick up the card until you say the answer.) If you do not know, use a strategy to figure it out. Find a way to figure out how many squares there are without counting every one.

3 Turn the card over to check your answer. If your answer is correct, keep the card.

4 If you are playing with a partner, take turns choosing cards and finding the number of squares in each array. Play until you have picked up all the cards.

5 While you are playing, make lists for yourself of "Combinations I Know" and "Combinations I'm Working On." You will be using these lists to help you learn your multiplication combinations.

Fraction Cookie (page 1 of 2)

You need

- pattern blocks
- fraction number cubes (2 in one color and 1 in a different color)
- *Hexagon Cookies*

Play with a partner or in a group.

1 Each player rolls one fraction number cube and takes that amount in pattern blocks, or "cookies." Record the cookies you collect on *Hexagon Cookies.*

2 At the end of a turn, each player must have the fewest number of pieces possible. For example, if you have $2\frac{1}{2}$ cookies altogether, you should have 2 yellows and 1 red in front of you. Trade in smaller fraction pieces for larger ones, and check each other's cookie shares as you play.

3 Take turns and collect cookies until you have filled in the sheet. The player who finishes first wins.

Fraction Cookie (page 2 of 2)

Intermediate: Adding Fraction Cookies
(two fraction number cubes)

Each player rolls two fraction number cubes, adds the two amounts, and collects that amount of cookies in pattern blocks. Continue to trade so that you always have the fewest pieces possible at the end of your turn. Play continues until players have filled up one sheet; players may also agree to fill two sheets in this version.

Advanced: Adding and Subtracting Fraction Cookies
(three fraction number cubes)

Each player rolls two fraction number cubes of one color and a third fraction number cube of a different color, adds the amounts on the first two cubes, and then subtracts the amount on the third cube from his or her cookie collection. Continue to trade so that you always have the fewest pieces possible at the end of your turn. In this version of the game, start with two whole hexagon cookies so you do not run out when you subtract. The first player to get four cookies (or any other number agreed on) wins.

Go Collecting (page 1 of 2)

You need

- deck of Collection Cards
- *Go Collecting* Recording Sheet

Play with a partner.

1 Deal five Collection Cards to each player. Place the remaining deck facedown on the table.

2 Each player takes a turn to try to match two Collection Cards that are in the same category. For example, if you have the Butterfly Collection Card (#17) and the Snake Collection Card (#19), which are both in the Animals category, then you have a match.

3 When it is your turn, if you have a pair of cards that match, place them faceup on the table and figure out how many hundreds you have altogether. Record the number of hundreds on the *Go Collecting* Recording Sheet.

Go Collecting (page 2 of 2)

4 If you do not have a pair when it is your turn, try to find one by asking your partner. For example, you can ask, "Kelly, do you have any Animal cards?" If your partner has a card that belongs to the category you named, he or she must give you that card. Then put the pair faceup on the table. Figure out how many hundreds are in the pair and record your score. If your partner does not have a card from the category you named, he or she will say, "Go Collecting!" Take a card from the deck. If you make a pair, figure out the number of hundreds and record your score. If not, your turn is over.

5 Each player may make only one pair on a turn. If you have more than one pair in your hand, save it for your next turn.

6 On each turn, the other player will also find the number of hundreds in the sum of your two collection cards. Compare solutions to make sure that your total is correct.

7 At the end of each turn, discard or draw cards to make sure that you have exactly five cards in your hand when you start your next turn.

8 Continue in turns until a player reaches 20 points. If you run out of cards in the deck, mix the cards in the discard pile and use them again.

How Far from 100?

You need

- deck of Digit Cards
- *How Far from 100?* Recording Sheet

Play in pairs.

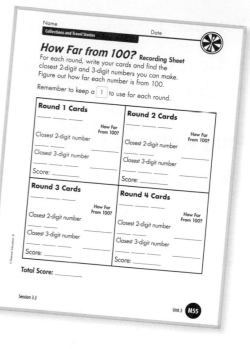

1 Give each player a 1 Digit Card from the deck to use throughout the game. Deal three Digit Cards to each player.

1

2 Players use two of their cards to make a 2-digit number as close to 100 as possible. Players write their 2-digit numbers and how far their numbers are from 100 on the recording sheet. Players discuss whether they have made the closest 2-digit numbers possible.

3 Players then choose from the same 3 cards they were dealt, plus the 1 they were given at the beginning of the game, and make the closest possible 3-digit number to 100. Players write their 3-digit numbers and how far their numbers are from 100 on the recording sheet. Players discuss whether they have made the closest 3-digit numbers possible.

4 Players find their scores by determining which distance is closest to 100. For example, if Player 1's 2-digit number is 14 away from 100, and Player 1's 3-digit number is 32 away from 100, then Player 1's score for that round is 14.

5 Each player puts the three cards they were dealt in a discard pile, keeping the 1 card for the rest of the rounds.

6 Play continues for a total of four rounds, repeating Steps 1–5 each time.

7 Players total their scores for the 4 rounds. The player with the lowest score wins.

Make a Dollar

You need

- Coin Cards (deck of 32)
- *Make a Dollar* Recording Sheet

Play with one or two other players.

1 Deal eight Coin Cards faceup. Put the rest of the deck in a pile facedown.

2 Player 1 finds all pairs of cards that equal a dollar and records the equation for each pair on the *Make a Dollar* Recording Sheet.

3 When there are no more pairs that make a dollar, Player 2 draws new cards from the deck to replace the cards Player 1 used. Each player should start with eight cards.

4 Any time all players agree that no combinations of the eight cards make a dollar, shuffle all eight cards back into the deck and deal eight new cards.

5 The goal is to collect as many pairs of cards (dollars) as possible. The game ends when all the cards have been paired.

Scoring Variation

Make combinations of cards that equal any whole number of dollars. For example, a player could take three cards with 50¢, 70¢, and 80¢ for a total of two dollars. Your score at the end of the game is the number of dollars you have collected.

Missing Factors (page 1 of 2)

You need

- set of Array Cards
- *Missing Factors* Recording Sheet

Play alone or with a partner. This game is a variation of Factor Pairs.

 Spread out all of the Array Cards in front of you with the product side up.

 Choose an Array Card. One dimension is written for you. The *missing factor* is the other dimension. You must say what the missing factor is. For example, if you choose an Array Card that has the product of 16, and one dimension is 2, the missing factor is 8.

16	2

 Turn the card over to check your answer. If your answer is correct, keep the card. If your answer is not correct, return the card to the set of Array Cards, dimensions side up.

Missing Factors (page 2 of 2)

4 On the *Missing Factors* Recording Sheet, write an equation to go with each array you keep. Circle the missing factor. For example:

$2 \times \boxed{8} = 16$ or $16 \div 2 = \boxed{8}$

5 If you are playing with a partner, take turns choosing cards until all the cards with products still showing have been picked up.

6 When there are only cards with dimensions sides showing, take turns pointing to a card and saying what is on the other side (the product), keeping the cards when your answers are correct. The player with the most cards wins.

Practicing with Multiplication Cards

(page 1 of 2)

You need

- 6 sheets of Multiplication Cards
- Array Cards
- scissors
- paper clip
- resealable plastic bag

Play with a partner.

1 Cut out each Multiplication Card and write your initials and the product on the back. Check each product with a calculator, your Array Cards, or someone else's help.

2 Ask someone to show you the front of each Multiplication Card. Say the product as quickly as you can. If you get it right away, put the card in a pile of combinations that you "just know." If you have to stop and figure it out, put it into a different pile of combinations that you are "working on."

3 Paper clip your "just know" cards together and put them in the plastic bag.

Practicing with Multiplication Cards

(page 2 of 2)

 Look at each card in your "working on" pile. Think of an easy multiplication combination that you already know that can help you remember this one. Write it on the line that says "Start with _____."

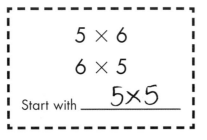

5×6

6×5

Start with ___5×5___

5 Practice each of the cards in your "working on" pile at least three times.

6 Put all your cards back together (including the ones you "just know") and go through them again. Keep practicing over the next few weeks until you have no more cards in your "working on" pile.

What's My Shape?

You need

- *Geometric Solids*

Play with a partner.

1 Choose a secret polyhedron (a shape with flat sides only) from the shapes on *Geometric Solids.*

2 Write the name of the polyhedron you chose on the back of this sheet or on another sheet of paper.

3 Write a description of the solid that will help someone guess the polyhedron you chose. Write at least two characteristics of your solid.

For example: My polyhedron has exactly 6 square faces and 8 corners. (My polyhedron is a cube.)

Illustrations

Photographs